Best
Friends
Forever

Me and My
Cat

Living with animals can be a wonderful experience, especially if we choose to learn the valuable lessons animals teach through their natural enthusiasm, grace, resourcefulness, affection and forgiveness.

Richard H. Pitcairn

Best Friends Forever

Me and My Cat

What I've Learned
About **Life**, **Love**, and **Faith**
From My Cat

BETHANYHOUSE
MINNEAPOLIS, MINNESOTA

Best Friends Forever: Me and My Cat
What I've Learned About Life, Love, and Faith From My Cat
Copyright © 2010 by GRQ, Inc.
Brentwood, Tennessee 37027

Scripture quotations noted CEV are from THE CONTEMPORARY ENGLISH VERSION. Copyright 1991, 1992, 1995 by the American Bible Society. Used by permission.

Scripture quotations noted ESV are from THE ENGLISH STANDARD VERSION. Copyright © 2001 b Crossway Bibles, a division of Good News Publishers.

Scripture quotations noted MSG are from THE MESSAGE. Copyright © 1993, 1994, 1995, 1996, 200 2001, 2002. Used by permission of NavPress Publishing Group.

Scripture quotations noted NIV are from the HOLY BIBLE: NEW INTERNATIONAL VERSIO▮ (North American Edition)®. Copyright © 1973, 1978, 1984, by the International Bible Society. Used b permission of Zondervan. All rights reserved.

Scripture quotations noted NKJV are from THE NEW KING JAMES VERSION. Copyright © 1979, 198 1982, Thomas Nelson, Inc., Publishers.

Scripture quotations noted NLT are from the HOLY BIBLE: NEW LIVING TRANSLATION, copyright ▮ 1996, 2004. Used by permission of Tyndale House Publishers, Inc., Wheaton, Illinois 60189. All righ▮ reserved.

Published by Bethany House Publishers
11400 Hampshire Avenue South
Bloomington, Minnesota 55438

Bethany House Publishers is a division of
Baker Publishing Group, Grand Rapids, Michigan.

ISBN-13: 978-0-7642-0774-7

Editor: Lila Empson Wavering
Associate Editor: Natasha Sperling
Manuscript written and compiled by Patricia R. Mitchell in association with Snapdragon Group[SM]
Design: Whisner Design Group

Printed in the United States of America

When you're special to a cat,
you're special indeed.
She brings to you the gift of her
preference of you, the sight of you,
the sound of your voice,
the touch of your hand.

Leonore Fleisher

Contents

Introduction

I have felt cats rubbing their faces against mine and touching my cheek with claws carefully sheathed. These things, to me, are expressions of love.

James Herriot

From earliest times, cats have enchanted cat lovers with their mysterious beauty, agile grace, contemplative gaze, and comforting presence. Anyone whose life has been blessed with a cat's special love knows the pleasure of stroking a cat's lush fur, pondering a cat's unspoken thoughts, and dozing to the rhythmic rumble of a cat's contented purr.

My first cat came into my life on my twelfth birthday, and there have been few years since then that I have been without a companion cat—or several companion cats. Each of my current feline friends, along with each of those whose memories live in my heart, possesses a distinct personality and unique temperament, and each cat has brought its own particular grace and happiness into my life.

Though cats are commonly portrayed as snooty, standoffish, and self-sufficient, anyone privileged to receive a cat's affection knows those words do not describe their beloved feline friend. On the contrary, cats, like humans, yearn for the presence of another living being and the warmth of another's love. Domestic cats depend on our care for their shelter, safety, and well-being, and in return offer us a lifetime of genuine devotion and a treasure of cherished memories. Cats, just by being themselves, show us how to enjoy the day's simple pleasures, overcome obstacles with courage and resourcefulness, rest without worry about tomorrow, and navigate every season of life with poise and elegance.

Best Friends Forever: Me and My Cat is a collection of stories inspired by the many cats that have come into my life and into the lives of friends, colleagues, and fellow church members. Each one of us has found in the cats we have known a touch of God's comfort, a glimpse of his smile, an appreciation of his creative hand through the presence and affection of our beloved cats.

I invite you to curl up with your favorite feline and allow these stories to touch and inspire you, comfort and encourage you, and even make you laugh. Share with me the heartwarming moments, the simple wisdom, the daily joys of cat lovers everywhere whose hearts have been touched by the life, love, and *purrrfect* friendship of their beloved cats.

To some blind souls, all cats are much alike. To a cat lover, every cat from the beginning of time has been utterly and amazingly unique.

Jenny de Vries

Paws in Traffic

He that does good to another does good also to
himself, not only in the consequence but
in the very act. For the consciousness of
well-doing is in itself ample reward.

Seneca

When it comes to accepting God's love, some people ask, "Why me? What have I done to deserve God's love, or his mercy, or his forgiveness?" To these people I say, "Let me tell you about the scruffy kittens my colleague Stephanie rescued." These helpless orphans never pulled back to question why Stephanie rescued them from the street, but instead they happily accepted their newfound prosperity.

Before leaving for work one morning, Stephanie glanced out her living room window and saw kittens frolicking in the street in front of her house. A tipped-over cardboard box lay at the curb, and it appeared the kittens had scampered out of the box and were now exploring the middle of the street, heedless of danger.

Stephanie dashed outside, grabbed the box, and scooped up

the kittens as quickly as she could—one, two, three, four, five in all! Stephanie noticed the kittens were dirty and infested with fleas, but she had only ten minutes before she needed to leave for work. She put the tiny creatures in the bathtub with a bowl of water, shut the bathroom door, and left for the office. The rescued kittens became the topic of the day's conversation, and cat lover and colleague Eva agreed to go to Stephanie's house after work and help her decide what to do with the five orphans.

> *I love cats. I have a lot of cat tales . . . so to speak. A lot of my cats come to me. They show up at my house. I'm kind of a cat lady that way.*
> **Gina Gershon**

Mewling, dirty, scrawny, and covered with fleas, the kittens did not look pretty. By Eva's estimation, they were under six weeks old, too young to have been separated from their mother, and might have behavioral problems later on. Nonetheless, Stephanie and Eva cleaned the kittens as best they could and found food for them to eat.

Eva picked the tortoiseshell, which she named Sushi, to join her two adult cats at home. Stephanie chose one of the two black kittens, which she named Ebony, to stay in her home. So in the bathtub there remained three kittens: another black, a gray, and an orange striped. Stephanie decided to take them to work with her in the morning to see if any of her co-workers would take the others.

The next day, Stephanie placed a box containing three fed, comfortable, and playful kittens next to her desk, and a stream of co-workers came by as word of the kittens' presence spread throughout the office. Though Stephanie's supervisor viewed the kittens as a distraction, by five that afternoon, all three kittens had been claimed by a human and were on their way to a new life.

The black kitten went home with an artist, the gray kitten went home with an accounts manager, and the orange tabby came home with me. I named him Eli. Though Eva's Sushi suffered no ill effects of her precarious start in life, Eli grew into a feisty old tomcat, never developing the manners or temperament of a gentle house cat. Eli ate with the fervor of creatures that have once known hunger and developed a portly physique along the lines of Garfield. In Eli's later years, he regarded his litter box as one option among many, including behind the sofa or in the corner of a room. When either annoyed or playful, Eli bit and scratched—a behavior I thought cute from a wispy kitten, but less charming from an eighteen-pound tom. Despite his many quirks and foibles, Eli was loved dearly and remains in my heart as the granddaddy of all cats yet to come into my life.

> *Real love isn't our love for God, but his love for us. God sent his Son to be the sacrifice by which our sins are forgiven.*
> 1 John 4:10 CEV

Each kitten Stephanie rescued was chosen by a caring person and taken to a loving home. The kittens, though scrawny, flea-bitten, and of questionable parentage, did nothing to earn their good fortune, nor did their appearance or achievement attract special favor. Each was rescued and loved simply because people had compassion on the helpless creatures and opened their hearts and homes to them.

> *Remember that when you leave this earth, you can take with you nothing that you have received—only what you have given: a full heart, enriched by honest service, love, sacrifice and courage.*
>
> **Saint Francis of Assisi**

In the same way, God opens his heart and home to us, no matter where he finds us today, how we look, or what we have accomplished in life. He's not interested in those things. He has chosen us simply because he is a God of compassion and love, and he's going to do compassionate, merciful, and loving things, like take us into his heart just because he is God and we are who we are.

Where's Eli?

Places to look: behind the books in the book-shelf, any cupboard with a gap too small for any cat to squeeze through . . . under anything too low for a cat to squash under and inside the piano.

Roseanne Ambrose-Brown

Change brings stress. Even welcome change like graduation, marriage, or the birth of a baby causes tension until the days and weeks unfold and life resumes in a fairly predictable pattern. Those who adjust well to change are those who are able to tolerate uncertainty until they figure out the new rules, but cats are not in this group. Cats do not adjust well to change, as our big orange tom, Eli, demonstrated.

Eli came as a kitten to our condo, where he grew to a comfortable maturity as the only cat of the household. King of his territory, his humans, and his food bowl, Eli saw no need to change a thing. At a certain point, however, I decided I wanted a yard so I could garden, and when the house on a large lot next door to my sister's house went up for sale, my mother, brother, and I bought it.

His humans' sudden obsession with bringing boxes down from closet shelves raised Eli's suspicions. The cat grew more anxious as small tables and bookcases disappeared, leaving empty corners in need of serious sniffing for clues as to their whereabouts. Then when moving day came, Eli found himself in his carrier and crammed in the backseat of the car along with houseplants, and he spit, growled, and howled his displeasure for ten long miles.

> *A home without a cat, and a well-fed, well-petted and properly revered cat, may be a perfect home, perhaps, but how can it prove its title?*
> Mark Twain

At our new house, I set up Eli with his food, litter box, and familiar blanket in a bathroom until the movers brought in the big furniture and we were able to close the outside doors. When I opened the bathroom door, I found a timid, fearful, wide-eyed Eli, unwilling to cross the threshold of his tiny tiled haven of safety. I decided to let him discover the house on his own terms, and I went about unpacking boxes, hanging up clothes, and arranging furniture. By evening, Eli was nowhere to be found.

We looked everywhere. I fretted, sure he had gotten outside and was now trying to find his way back to our house. "He couldn't have gotten out," my mother assured me. "We haven't opened any doors since you let him out of the bathroom." Nonetheless,

I had heard those stories of cats showing up months, even years later at their old homes, but there was nothing I could do except ask neighbors to let me know if they spotted a big orange tomcat wandering around.

A few days after our move, and still no Eli, I decided the electric organ, housed in a heavy, old-fashioned console, would look better in another room, and two friends agreed to move it for me. "Hey, did you know there's a cat in here?" one of them asked. I peered way back behind the pedals of the organ, and there sat Eli, hunched, silent, the massive console protecting him against all comers.

Eli's fear caused him to seek refuge in a small, cramped place where we couldn't easily find him. It took patient coaxing with food and soothing words before Eli ventured out of the place he had picked as a fortress against the change that had taken his familiar territory away from him. Once Eli stepped out from the organ's maw, however, he discovered a whole new kingdom to call his own.

"Can anyone hide in secret places so that I cannot see him?" declares the LORD. "Do not I fill heaven and earth?" declares the LORD.
Jeremiah 23:24 NIV

Eli's fearful reaction to a change in territory is not unlike a human's natural reaction to the changes life brings, particularly life's unpleasant changes, such as loss, bereavement, illness, or injury.

Suddenly we find ourselves in an alien place filled with uncertainties, and we're not sure where familiar markers are, or even if those markers still exist. Instead of stepping out into our new world, however, we tend to want to stay in the past and protect ourselves against our new surroundings.

I am the creator of my life and my world. I meet daily challenges gracefully and with complete confidence. I fill my mind with positive, nurturing, and healing thoughts.
Alice Potter

If life is changing in ways we don't understand right now, we may wish we could crawl into a dark corner until things go back to the way they were. They won't, though, and God may be using change to move us to a new place, a place he has filled with blessings we have yet to discover. He can coax us out of our hiding place and show us the new and renewed life he has planned for us.

Left Behind

It is the LORD who goes before you.
He will be with you; he will
not leave you or forsake you.
Do not fear or be dismayed.
Deuteronomy 31:8 ESV

Sometimes we find ourselves wandering in a spiritual desert. Our prayers disappear into a dry, unhearing wind, and the presence of God seems a mirage in the distance. We feel abandoned by God, but in truth, God has not abandoned us because God never abandons his own. God acts in sharp contrast to people who decide to move on and leave a living being behind.

Angie, a college student, lived in an apartment near her university, and during the summer while she traveled, she sublet the space. The arrangement worked well for the first two summers, but at the end of the third summer, she returned home to find her apartment still occupied. As Angie opened the door, she was met by the sound of plaintive meows and the sight of a tiny four-footed creature, a puffball of fur, edging cautiously toward her.

Surprise gave way to anger. Clearly, the kitten had been abandoned and closed in the apartment for several days without food or water. The kitten's plight silenced any thoughts on Angie's part of contacting the sublessee about his "loss," and Angie took immediate responsibility for the kitten by dashing to the grocery store for several cans of cat food. The kitten bolted down the first bowlful Angie set out.

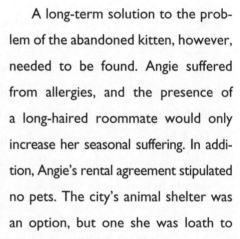

It is impossible for a lover of cats to banish these alert, gentle, and discriminating friends, who give us just enough of their regard and complaisance to make us hunger for more.
Agnes Repplier

A long-term solution to the problem of the abandoned kitten, however, needed to be found. Angie suffered from allergies, and the presence of a long-haired roommate would only increase her seasonal suffering. In addition, Angie's rental agreement stipulated no pets. The city's animal shelter was an option, but one she was loath to choose. So Angie did what any woman knows to do when faced with one of life's dilemmas: She phoned her girlfriend.

Alarie, a cat lover and fellow student of Angie's who lived nearby, came immediately when she heard the words "abandoned kitten." Arriving at Angie's apartment, Alarie swooped up the creature in her arms and let him rub his face against her shoulder as he purred nonstop. "I think he's a Maine coon," Alarie announced as she examined his unusually long and bushy tail, shaggy coat, and mottled brown markings, "and he's starved for attention."

"He's starved for food, too," said Angie, pointing to the licked-clean bowl as she opened another can of cat food. "So what are we going to do? I can't keep him here."

"I'll take him," Alarie announced without hesitation. At the sound of more food being spooned into his bowl, the kitten scampered from Alarie's arms and dug into his second helping.

"You can't have pets in your apartment," Angie reminded her.

"True, but he's going with me anyway. Call me a criminal," said the heretofore law-abiding citizen. The kitten, having eaten too much too fast, vomited on the carpet.

Alarie smuggled the kitten into her apartment, named him Strauss, and managed to keep him under the property owner's radar until graduation, when she and the now-husky adult cat

> *You will never find Jesus so precious as when the world is one vast howling wilderness. Then he is like a rose blooming in the midst of the desolation, a rock rising above the storm.*
> **Robert Murray M'Cheyne**

relocated into a pet-friendly apartment near Alarie's first job. A few years later, Chris, Alarie's husband, joined the household, and Strauss took immediately to his second source of food, love, and cuddles.

Though Strauss lived a full eighteen years under the faithful and loving care of Alarie and Chris, the cat never forgot the trauma

> *Frequently remind yourself that God is with you, that he will never fail you, that you can count upon him. Say these words, "God is with me, helping me."*
> Norman Vincent Peale

he suffered when he was left behind in an empty apartment with no food, water, or companionship. At every meal, Strauss ate ravenously, even after he had no reason to doubt the appearance and abundance of his next dish.

Whenever Alarie and Chris packed for a weekend away, Strauss spread his bulk over their suitcases and pleaded with his big Maine coon eyes for them to stay home, never mind their reliable cat-sitter who checked in on him during the day. The fear of being left behind in a silent, friendless, and foodless desert had imprinted itself on his soul.

During times of spiritual dryness, we need to remind ourselves that, unlike people, God will never abandon us. He remains faithful, even when the human heart and mind leave him behind in pursuit of other pleasures. As he was faithful to us yesterday, he remains faithful to us today, and he will be faithful to us tomorrow. We will never be left behind by God.

A Healing Hand

I soon realized the name Pouncer in no way did justice to her aerial skills. By the end of the first day I had amended her name to Kamikaze.

Cleveland Amory

Many of us carry visible scars left by long-ago physical injuries, and many more of us live with the invisible wounds of past emotional trauma. With time, support, and compassion, our hearts' wounds may diminish in intensity, but rarely do these scars disappear entirely from memory, soul, and spirit. Sometimes those wounds color perception and behavior, as is the case with Juno, the cat who had a rough start in life.

My sister, Janice, who has long favored Siamese cats, learned of a Siamese kitten named Juno who was in desperate need of a new home. "The first time I saw Juno," Janice said, "she was sitting in a window of the apartment belonging to Sharon, the woman who had her up for adoption. Juno was beautiful, a classic seal point, dainty and svelte. She seemed calm and friendly, even playing with a ball of aluminum foil while Sharon told me about her."

One of Sharon's girlfriends had received Juno as a gift shortly after the kitten's birth, and the young woman did not treat Juno very well. She often neglected to refill the kitten's food bowl or give her fresh water. "I'd go over there," Sharon explained, "and sometimes there'd be nothing out for her to eat or drink, and her litter box would need cleaning."

Sharon told my sister that the woman's boyfriend teased Juno and played roughly with her, so Juno spent a lot of time huddled under the bed or a couch, trying to stay out of sight.

> *He has become a much better cat than I have a person. With his gentle urgings, he made me realize that life doesn't end just because one has a few obstacles to overcome.*
> Mary F. Graf

"I kept telling my friend to give Juno up for adoption because she wasn't living a lifestyle that accommodated a cat," Sharon said, "and she finally agreed when she bought new living room furniture and didn't want cat hair on it. So I took Juno home with me, and now I'd like to find a good home for her rather than take her to the shelter. She's such a pretty little thing."

Janice thanked the woman for looking after Juno's well-being and agreed to give the exquisite Siamese a permanent home. When Juno realized another change was about to take place, the serene goddess of catdom vanished, and a frightened, fighting ball of teeth and claws emerged. Once secured in the car, Juno yowled at an earsplitting pitch all the way to Janice's house, and once inside her new home, Juno surveyed her surroundings with deep suspicion. Juno hissed and backed away in self-defense when Janice's husband offered her a gentle touch of welcome.

During those first few months, Juno earned a reputation as the world's meanest cat, a reputation she has yet to lose completely. She springs at any passing leg with all claws bared, and pounces on the toes of any hapless visitor wearing sandals. Juno has no qualms about biting the hand that feeds her, even once biting Janice on her nose, leaving Janice, a teacher, to explain to both colleagues and class how she happened to come

> *Be still before the LORD and wait patiently for him; fret not yourself over the one who prospers in his way, over the man who carries out evil devices! Refrain from anger, and forsake wrath!*
> Psalm 37:7–8 ESV

to school with teeth marks on the end of her nose. "Early on, people thought we ought to get rid of her," Janice said. "Even the vet told me she might be too wild to keep."

Time passed, and Juno slowly responded to the loving care she received from her new family and her steady supply of savory food and clean water. Freedom from torment worked to calm her nerves, build her trust in humans, and heal the wounds left from her rocky start in life. Though Juno remains most decidedly "Janice's cat," she accepts the attention of Janice's husband and the presence of visitors if they keep a respectful distance. Having too many people in the house, however, agitates Juno, and the cat's wary eyes tell that she still remembers.

> *The past is finished.*
> *There is nothing to be*
> *gained by going over*
> *it. Whatever it gave us*
> *in the experiences it*
> *brought us was some-*
> *thing we had to know.*
> Rebecca Beard

We, too, are unlikely to forget a trauma that ripped a life apart, a sorrow that put an end to happiness, a grief that drained a soul's peace. Yet with the passing of time and the steady and reliable love of others, our wounds heal, our scars diminish, and we learn to trust again. In healing, we find our hope and our happiness renewed, and when we do, we rediscover that God is our Great Physician, not only of body, but of heart, soul, and spirit, as well.

All the Difference

We ourselves feel that what we are doing is just a drop in the ocean. But the ocean would be less because of that missing drop.

Mother Teresa

According to the story, a boy was walking along the shore where starfish had been washed up by the tide, and he began returning some of them to the ocean. An observer chuckled and said, "Do you really think you're making a difference?" As the boy placed another starfish in the water, he replied, "I'm sure making a difference to this one." The boy's attitude is a good one to remember at the animal shelter.

After our home was left catless by the passing of Eli, our big orange tom, my brother and I visited our local animal shelter to pick out another feline companion for our family. After entering the drab, shabby building that houses our city's homeless dogs and cats, we were ushered back to a clean but stark room with several rows of kennels stacked against two walls, each one holding a kitten or cat.

"I wish we could take them all," my brother remarked.

"Me, too," I said as I approached the first row of cages. I received varied levels of interest from many of the cats, but by far the cat most eager to have me stop by was a rather scruffy, yet alert and energetic, calico. "Callie," her nameplate announced, "two and one-half years old, domestic longhair." I was looking for a grown cat, so her age was in her favor, and I was intrigued by Callie's calico coat, her patches reminding me of a scrap quilt. Wanting to give each cat a chance, however, I moved from Callie's cage to visit her neighbors, and when I did, Callie retreated to the back of her kennel. When I returned to Callie, she again sprang to attention and put her nose right up to the front of the bars. Clearly, Callie was going home with me.

> *Four little Persians,*
> *but only one looked*
> *in my direction. I*
> *extended a tentative*
> *finger and two soft*
> *paws clung to it. There*
> *was a contented sound*
> *of purring, I suspect*
> *on both our parts.*
> George Freedley

Meanwhile, my brother was strolling along the rows of cages, with no particular intention of picking out a cat (he had left that job to me), when the claws of a tiny gray paw grabbed a leg of his jeans. A tabby kitten, marked with gray and black stripes and a white button in the middle of her chest, was determined to get his attention by frolicking at the front of her cage and reaching out as far as her little paws would go. "Buttercup," her nameplate said, "six months old, domestic shorthair." My brother and I adopted both cat and kitten, exhilarated at the prospect of rescuing these two needy animals, but sad, too, at having to leave the rest of the cats behind.

Buttercup, who became Cup in our house, adjusted quite quickly, perhaps because of her youth. Callie, however, hid under my bed for a week or so, edgy and suspicious, until I finally decided it was time to drag her out, and I did. She was as skinny and ill-groomed as she had been in the

> *My beloved brethren, be steadfast, immovable, always abounding in the work of the Lord, knowing that your labor is not in vain in the Lord.*
> **1 Corinthians 15:58**
> NKJV

shelter, and I was determined to show Callie that she had chosen for herself a good home and kindly humans. After several days of hand-feeding, petting, brushing, holding, and cuddling, Callie at last began to groom herself. She ventured out of my bedroom and explored the rest of the house, found her own way to the food and water, and began to fill out in short order. In the meantime, Callie made it clear to Cup that there was a hierarchy in effect, and Cup was number two. Callie proclaimed herself reigning cat of the two-cat household, and she staked her claim to my lap as her exclusive property.

At the shelter, Callie and Cup were among dozens of cats and kittens needing a home, and as much as my brother and I wish we could have provided for all of them, we were able to rescue only two. Maybe our help didn't make much difference to the nation's homeless cat population, but we know for certain we made a big difference in the lives of two.

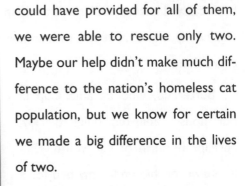

I hope to make people realize how totally helpless animals are, how dependent on us, trusting as a child must that we will be kind and take care of their needs.

James Herriot

When we feel overwhelmed by the many needs of the world, we need to remember we can make a difference—not to the whole world, but to one cat, one family member, one friend, one stranger. And to that one soul, we have made all the difference in the world.

Mixed Signals

Friendship, which is of its nature a delicate thing, fastidious, slow of growth, is easily checked, will hesitate, demure, recoil where love, good old blustering love, bowls ahead and blunders through every obstacle.

Colette

Body language plays a vital role in communication among humans, and also in communication between humans and felines. Cats pick up human body language instantly, especially movements preceding the preparation of food, and it's for humans to know what a cat means when she sits stonily in front of an empty bowl and glares. Miscommunication happens, however, when humans—or cats—misread signals.

From kittenhood, Cup never seemed in need of special attention. While Cup tolerated a few head-to-tail strokes (more to please me than anything else, I suspect), she refused to sit still for brushing. When I picked her up, she'd leap off my lap as soon as I relaxed my grip, then indignantly lick herself where my hands had touched her. I drew the conclusion she didn't like me and would rather I keep my hands and my scent to myself. *I prefer my own fragrance, thank you very much*, Cup's body language blared. Cup's fragrance of choice reapplied, she would trot off, throwing a furtive look back at me to make sure I was making no move to pick her up again. I would have liked to hold her, but I can respect the pride and preferences of a cat. I must admit, however, the unambiguous meaning of Cup's body language hurt my feelings.

> *A purring cat is a form of high praise, like a gold star on a test paper. It is reinforcement for something we would all like to believe about ourselves — that we are nice.*
> Roger A. Caras

Cup's wariness of close human contact continued over time, and I began to wonder if she associated being picked up with having a pill popped into her mouth. Shortly after Cup came to live with us, she developed a bladder infection, for which the vet prescribed a capsule to be given daily. Anyone who has tried to induce an unwilling cat to swallow a pill knows that it happens only if the cat's mouth can be pried open, the pill inserted in the throat, and the neck massaged until the pill is swallowed—or maybe swallowed. During the course of Cup's treatment, I found soggy gel capsules stuck on upholstery, floors, and the front of my T-shirt hours after I thought Cup had swallowed her dosage for the day. Cup's discomfort with being picked up could certainly stem from her traumatic experience with pills. "She needs to associate my touch with something pleasant," I decided.

I began slowly, as is best when trying to establish new habits and new associations. While she ate, I stroked her several times, talked soothingly to her, and then left the room. No pickup, no pills. I began brushing her lightly, gradually lengthening the time I spent with her. Cup eyed me warily at first, but then seemed to find some

> *Be wise in the way you act toward outsiders; make the most of every opportunity. Let your conversation be always full of grace, seasoned with salt, so that you may know how to answer everyone.*
> **Colossians 4:5–6** NIV

pleasure in the exercise, and in her own time she relaxed and stretched out to invite a more thorough petting, including tummy and tail.

From stroking, brushing, and petting, I progressed to encircling Cup with my arms as she lay on the bed or a chair. She accepted the gesture and did not respond by immediately licking herself free of my scent. Then I felt the time was right to start picking her up and holding her in my lap. Cup stayed in my lap a millisecond, then a full second, then several seconds, and then longer. While by no means a lap cat, Cup now reads my body language not as preparation for capture, but as a desire to show affection. It took plain English, however, for me to read her after-touch licking as anything short of disdain.

While reading an article about cat behavior, I discovered that cats calm themselves by licking themselves, and my early attempts to cuddle Cup made her nervous, not nauseous. Clearly, we had misread each other's body language, as Cup saw my outstretched arms as a pill aimed for her throat, and I interpreted her self-soothing gesture as a rejection.

> *Remember not only to say the right thing, in the right place, but far more difficult still to leave unsaid the wrong thing at the tempting moment.*
> Benjamin Franklin

Body language—posture, gestures, nods, winks, grimaces—can signal genuine feelings and emotions, but can be as easily misunderstood as the spoken word. When someone's body language leaves us feeling hurt, troubled, or puzzled, it helps to find out for sure what that person meant to convey. Patience, willingness to give and take, and compassionate listening remain the surest ways to keep communication open, to please God, and to bring blessings to us and those we love.

The Newcomer

You know, we're all going in the same direction, or at least trying to. So we need to live together, get along together, and give each other enough space to be comfortable on that road.

Lillian Gideon

The scrawny calico captured my heart, and the gray tabby kitten peered up with pleading eyes as she clung to my brother's jeans. That day at the animal shelter, we adopted the pair of them. "There's room enough for you both," I assured Callie and Cup as I slipped the shelter's "I Have a Home" tags across their cages.

The two shelter cats may have preferred that only one of them gained a home that day, because, once home, they avoided each other for several weeks. In time, however, Callie and Cup accepted each other's presence and even started hanging around together. Like many cat lovers, however, I soon succumbed once more to the lure of a furry face. A photo in the newspaper's up-for-adoption column featured Indy, an elegant white longhair with ginger cap and tail. "It says she gets along well with other cats," I assured Callie and Cup, "and we have room for one more." The resident cats looked skeptical as I picked up my purse and left for the animal shelter.

Maybe it was no lie to say that Indy got along well with other cats, but no one thought to ask whether other cats got along well with Indy. Indy's sudden appearance did not amuse Callie and Cup, and they were in no mood to get along with her at all. Both of them divas, they responded with high emotion and unambiguous judgment: This territory has been taken.

> *Cats are beautiful, smart, perverse, outrageous, funny, and satisfying. They are probably the best of all creatures. Cats first, then people, and everything else comes after that. I definitely will get another one.*
> **Helen Gurley Brown**

Callie appeared the moment Indy arrived. She trotted into the kitchen, where Indy, just released from the cat carrier, sat in the center of the room surveying her surroundings with a bewildered expression on her face. Puzzled stranger and wary resident locked eyes. Callie reared, hissed, snarled, and positioned herself for a fight she clearly intended to win. I picked up Indy. This meeting was not off to a good start.

Cup, snoozing in her favorite spot in the living room when the commotion in the kitchen erupted, raised her head, sniffed the air, and slunk upstairs without even a glance at Indy. Cup settled herself, paws tucked tight to her body, on the corner of a bed where she could survey the doorway, alert for any further surprises, resistant to my attempts to coax her back downstairs to actually meet Indy.

Beloved, let us love one another, for love is from God, and whoever loves has been born of God and knows God. Anyone who does not love does not know God, because God is love.
1 John 4:7–8 ESV

That evening, I set up Indy in her own room and closed the door. Surely, I reasoned, Indy would be integrated into the family in a couple of days. But Cup continued to keep vigil from her bed-perch, and Callie remained livid with rage. *How could you do this to me? I deign to put up with the striped gray one, and now this affront to my sovereignty?* Callie threw me slit-eyed insults while swishing her now-formidable tail as she sniffed at the door to Indy's room.

Days passed as Cup guarded and Callie sulked. I stroked them, cuddled them, and talked to them in a soothing, reassuring voice. Finally, they reached the conclusion that Indy in no way compromised the level of love, food, space, and attention available to them. Cup presented herself downstairs and reclaimed her place in the household. Callie, not about to let the matter drop completely, still throws an occasional hiss in Indy's direction, but is reconciled to her presence. The three cats, even after the addition of yet another cat, often spend the day soaking in the sunshine by

Miss no single opportunity of making some small sacrifice, here by a smiling look, there by a kindly word; always doing the smallest right and doing it all for love.
Saint Thérèse of Lisieux

the same window in the same room. I like to think they've completely forgotten who came first, second, third, or fourth, and simply accept one another because they're all here and there's room enough for everyone.

When we're the newcomer, we can relate to Indy's trials. It's lonely until time and familiarity weave the bonds of friendship and shared experience, until the phone starts ringing and we find our name on the group e-mail list. It's a blessing when others stop regarding us as the newcomer and begin sharing their dreams and laughter, their hopes and joys, and everyone realizes that there's plenty of friendship to go around. And maybe a newcomer in our life would bless us forever for making room for one more friend today.

The Purr-pose Driven Cat

Unlike dogs, eager to make themselves indispensable to their human companions, a cat feels no need to please. Confident of her entitlements, a cat expects full service and will be clear about it if something falls short of complete satisfaction. Indy, however, proved herself the exception to the rule. She carved her niche in the family by being useful.

Indy entered a household dominated by two queenly cats, Callie and Cup. Shortly after Indy's arrival, the family increased by one more when Smokey made herself at home. Smokey, like Callie and Cup, put herself forward as one meriting all services due a cat of consequence.

In contrast to the other cats' haughty ways, Indy took the humble route. She neither howled for service nor vied for status, but quietly and gratefully took whatever was offered to her in the way of food and attention. Then she went about her business, which meant locating a warm and comfortable place to sleep. Unfortunately, couch, chairs, beds, and lounge were all spoken for, and she was growled off any soft surface occupied even infrequently by one of the other cats, whether the other cat wanted it at that moment or not. But human laps remained available, as none of the others took any interest in laps. This is where Indy found her comfort and refuge, and where she made herself useful.

> *Why do I like cats?*
> *They're capable of*
> *being very loyal and*
> *forming what passes for*
> *an emotional attach-*
> *ment without giving in*
> *totally and losing any-*
> *thing of themselves.*
> Marcia Muller

In my household, there are three human laps available: my mother's, my brother John's, and my own. Indy found most desirable the lap of our mother, whose daytime napping hours closely match a cat's, as Mom has seen many birthdays. Indy quickly learned to identify the movements and noises that precipitated a long, comfortable rest on Mom's warm and welcoming body—the squeak of the recliner, the shuffle of a blanket, the click of eyeglasses folded and placed on the table. Indy appears, stands at the ready, jumps into the embrace of Mom's arms, and begins her low, soft rumble of a purr until cat and Mom drop off to sound and peaceful sleep.

Indy likes to snuggle, so whenever John or I sit down to read or watch TV, Indy's sure to join one of us for strokes and a cuddle. She's a dependable lap cat, but her usefulness doesn't stop with laps. Her usefulness extends to far more gritty and practical matters.

> *I always pray with joy because of your partnership in the gospel . . . being confident of this, that he who began a good work in you will carry it on to completion until the day of Christ Jesus.*
> **Philippians 1:4–6** NIV

Late one autumn, as chilly winds brought a desire for warmth and coziness to cats and humans alike, a mouse got in the house. Was Callie, Cup, or Smokey worked up about it? Not at all. Apparently ease, contentment, and a never-empty food bowl have long separated them from the use their ancestors served in homes, barns, shops, factories, and ships. Those three cats were not about to get their paws mussed by meddling with a mouse. They merely watched as the rodent scampered across the floor. I leaped up onto the sofa and screeched.

Indy, however, sprang into action. Within seconds she had the rodent tracked, chased, cornered, and caught. Thank you, Indy! I was relieved that I didn't need to poke the mouse out from under the refrigerator or, worse yet, wonder where it had run off to. Later, after I had related all this to a friend, her young daughter declared, "Indy's a lap cat, a snuggle cat, a mouser cat—a multi-purpose cat!"

> A happy life is made up of little things—a gift sent, a letter written, a call made, a recommendation given, transportation provided, a cake made, a book lent, a check sent.
>
> Carol Holmes

The girl's apt observation brought to mind the value of humble people who quietly make themselves useful by doing small things. No extraordinary gifts required, only a willingness to see what needs doing and do it. Sometimes it takes no more than a warm smile or friendly greeting, and sometimes it costs a little time and effort.

When we do what needs doing, sometimes we'll get a round of applause from an admiring crowd. But most of the time we'll hear a simple "Thank you," and occasionally we won't hear anything at all. It doesn't matter. Whatever the response, we'll feel happy knowing we've taken care of one of the many needs in this world, and we'll give thanks to God, who has put each one of us here for a good and holy purpose.

Another cat? Perhaps. For love there is also a season; its seeds must be resown. But a family cat is not replaceable like a worn-out coat or a set of tires. Each new kitten becomes its own cat, and none is repeated. I am four cats old, measuring out my life in friends that have succeeded but not replaced one another.

Irving Townsend

Open, Please!

*Cats hate a closed door, you know,
regardless of which side they're on. If
they're out, they want to get in, and
if they're in, they want to get out.*
Lilian Jackson Braun

The saying goes, "When God closes one door he opens another." Callie is high-strung and behaves badly at closed doors. She'd never see God's open door because she'd be fixated on the door he closed. She'd scratch, claw, meow, and howl in front of the closed door while poking nose and paws underneath as far as possible and making life miserable for anyone who happened to be on the other side of that door.

Here's an example. Craving peace and quiet, I get a book, close my bedroom door, snuggle under a cozy throw, and settle down for a good read. Immediately, howling commences. Callie, sound asleep on the sofa just minutes ago, has discovered my whereabouts, and she's pitching a fit on the other side of my bedroom door. She's in no mood to look for another door, possibly because she's lived in the house long enough to know the room has only one door, and it's closed. *Waaahhh! Screeech! Scratch! Thump!* I put down my book, wriggle out from under the throw, and open the door.

My swift surrender to Callie's demand contrasts with the way God handles similar situations. He rarely shows himself such a pushover, no matter what antics I pull when confronted with a closed door. Now, maybe God intends for me to show some persistence, or perhaps he's holding out for evidence of strategic thinking. Of course, it might be he's telling me, "Get the message, girl. This is a closed door." In response, I think of a friend's opinion that when God closes one door, it's time to look for a window.

> *I have noticed that what cats most appreciate in a human being is not the ability to produce food, which they take for granted, but his or her entertainment value.*
> Geoffrey Household

Smokey looks for a window. The first time I saw her was the morning three years ago when I came into the kitchen and saw her sitting on the windowsill, looking in expectantly. I was startled, but Smokey acted as if it were the most natural thing in the world for her to be there. I cranked open the window and removed the screen, and Smokey jumped inside and demanded breakfast.

Most of the time Smokey lives happily as an indoor cat, but on occasion, twittering attractions in the yard call for a close-up-and-personal investigation. This is when she starts to poke around windows again. One day, she discovered a loose screen on the sun porch, pushed it open, and leaped outside. When I realized what had happened, I feared the worst, thinking I'd lost her and she'd never come back. But I fretted needlessly. Smokey showed up in her own good time on the sill of a second-story window, which, when opened, she slid right through, then pranced down to the kitchen and demanded dinner.

Look at me. I stand at the door. I knock. If you hear me call and open the door, I'll come right in and sit down to supper with you.
Revelation 3:20 MSG

Perseverance and strategic thinking certainly can work to open opportunities that, on first approach, appear closed. Cats tend to display these two characteristics. They also exhibit another characteristic. Upon gaining entrance to a room (by way of a door or window), they find they're not all that interested in it anyway.

Take Callie, for instance. After I get up and open the door for her, she sashays in, sniffs around for about ten seconds, then turns tail and leaves, completely dissatisfied with the room she had made such a fuss to enter.

God knows, too, there are some rooms even the most persistent knocker wouldn't like once inside, and some doors and windows the sharpest strategic thinking won't open. It's easy to keep knocking, keep probing, keep nagging, under the illusion there's some great and wonderful treasure on the other side of any given closed door. Not necessarily so.

Sometimes a closed door is a closed door, and windows are latched securely for good reason. This is when God says, "Look around and see the door I've opened for you! This is where I'm waiting for you!" When this happens, we can't be like Callie and continue caterwauling at the closed portal. We can't copy Smokey and attempt to maneuver our way in through some other opening. We can show our tails to the closed door, forget the windows, and prance proudly through the doors God holds wide open. We can stretch out languorously like cats who have found a banquet (because we have). We can enjoy the place our loving God has prepared for us.

> *When one door of happiness closes, another opens; but often we look so long at the closed door that we do not see the one which has been opened for us.*
> **Helen Keller**

The Real Thing or Nothing

As anyone who has ever been around a cat for any length of time well knows, cats have enormous patience with the limitations of the human mind.

Cleveland Amory

Most of us have experienced "information overload." We get news, commentary, and gossip from TV, radio, satellite, cell phone, and the Internet, a continuous stream of accurate data and deceptive statistics, scientific research and popular myth, timeless truths and fraudulent hoaxes. We're challenged to separate fact from fiction, something Sylvester the black-and-white camp cat had no trouble doing.

One weekend last fall, I went with friends from church to a nearby camp located in the Ozark Mountains. We stayed in the camp's newly built facility, complete with comfortable guest rooms, meeting rooms, an indoor pool, a dining room, and a chapel. Tall windows and balconies provided views of the woods, trails, and lake, offering a setting conducive to simply relaxing, chatting, and enjoying the quiet splendor of God's creation.

The first morning of our weekend, I got up just before dawn and slid the curtains away from the sliding glass door, hoping to step out onto the balcony and watch the sun rise over the lake. That's when I spotted movement: A small animal was moving out of the shadows and toward my door. Immediately, my imagination took over, and I mentally listed all the critters I thought might prowl in the predawn hours in the hills of the Ozarks. Porcupine. Raccoon. Woodchuck. Bear. As the creature drew closer, however, I discerned a familiar graceful gait and the silhouette of a long body, a long, swaying tail, and two dainty pointed ears. *Meow,* the creature said by way of greeting. I pulled open the door, and the cat walked in without hesitation.

> *Watch a cat when it enters a room for the first time. It searches and smells about, it is not quiet for a moment, it trusts nothing until it has examined and made acquaintance with everything.*
> **Jean-Jacques Rousseau**

The cat was a mature, easygoing tuxedo and obviously familiar with the routine of humans who wake up early in hopes of sitting out on the deck and watching the sunrise. My visitor dutifully accepted my words and strokes of greeting before hopping onto my bed, taking a bath, and curling up for a nap.

At breakfast, I learned from Nikki, our camp host, that the cat, Sylvester, at ten years old, was a lifelong resident of the camp and agreeable to all guests. (I also learned that my room faced west, so there would be no sunrise over the lake.) I enjoyed Sylvester's company during my weekend, and the cat quickly caught on that my door was always open to him.

> *We reject all shameful deeds and underhanded methods. We don't try to trick anyone or distort the word of God. We tell the truth before God, and all who are honest know this.*
> 2 Corinthians 4:2 NLT

The following spring, I returned to the camp for another event, and this time I came prepared for Sylvester's appearance and packed a bag of my four cats' favorite chicken-flavored treats and a yellow-gingham mouse for him to play with. As if he were expecting me, Sylvester appeared at my door, I slid it open, and the cat took his place on my bed and began bathing. Eager to please him, I opened the treats, a sound guaranteed to draw immediate attention at home, but Sylvester continued with his bath. I dropped a few chicken-flavored morsels beside him, and he stopped licking long enough to sniff these strange crumbs, then, uninterested, resumed his toilette.

I set the gingham mouse in front of him. Sylvester stopped his bath long enough to sniff the mouse, then, with a puzzled expression on his face, he looked up at me. *I get real chicken from the kitchen downstairs*, his stare explained, *so I don't want these pressed pellets, but if you'd like to nibble on them, go ahead. I don't mind. Same with the mouse. I get the real thing outside. After I've had a good nap, maybe I'll go out and get one for you. But in the meantime, you can take the gingham trinket and bat it around a little. Won't disturb me at all.* And with that, Sylvester curled up and went to sleep.

Sylvester's disinterest in anything less than the real thing reminded me that God has given me the "real thing" in his Word, the Bible. As he nourishes me with the heady food of his truth and draws me with the living spirit of his wisdom, he makes me dissatisfied with anything less than the genuine article. God's love for us is real, and his promises remain sure and certain. Why accept anything less?

> *The supreme end of education is expert discernment in all things—the power to tell the good from the bad, the genuine from the counterfeit, and to prefer the good and the genuine to the bad and the counterfeit.*
> **Samuel Johnson**

Fraidycat, Fearless Cat

Your cat may never have to hunt farther than the kitchen counter for its supper nor face a predator more fierce than the vacuum cleaner.

Barbara L. Diamond

Like humans, some cats flee at the faintest phantom of danger, while other cats (and humans) remain unmoved in the presence of obvious danger. One of our four indoor cats and an outdoor stray stand at opposite ends of the issue, approaching (or avoiding) the perils and predators of their lives in strikingly different ways, according to the level of audacity, daring, and courage each cat possesses.

Indy lives indoors and possesses nerves as delicate as her fluffy, dainty appearance might suggest. If I swoop a dust mop under the bed without looking first to see if Indy's there, and she is, she'll shoot out the other side of the bed as if I had pushed a pack of dogs under there. The mere sight of the vacuum puts Indy on high alert, and when I turn the vacuum on, Indy bolts from the room. Trouble is, she invariably seeks her safety in the next room

I'm headed to with the sweeper. Every vacuuming day, which is several days each week due to the presence of four shedding cats, a terrified Indy tries to flee the lumbering Goliath she believes is in pursuit of her.

The other three indoor cats take a wait-and-see approach when they hear me start the vacuum cleaner. If I bring it into a room where they've stretched out on the floor to sleep, the cats will seek high ground, such as a sofa, bed, or desk. As long as the machine keeps to the floor and makes no move toward them, the cats relax, though they keep watch just in case the situation should change.

Complete fearlessness is a trait of Gold Cat, the outdoor tabby. A rough-and-tumble tom, Gold Cat has

> *The cat has always been associated with the moon. Like the moon, it comes to life at night, escaping from humanity and wandering over housetops with its eyes beaming out through the darkness.*
> Patricia Dale-Green

been a presence in the neighborhood since kittenhood, before old age and illness curtailed his wanderings and confined him to a neighbor's home. Until that time, however, Gold Cat let nothing or no one intimidate him as he made his rounds from door to door, from garden to garden, across lawns and through hedges.

One morning while reaching for a bag of wild birdseed, I looked out the window and saw Gold Cat sitting serenely atop a low stone fence almost eyeball-to-eyeball with a mangy, hungry-looking coyote that was meandering only a few feet away from him. The tom was braver than I'll ever be, because when I saw the coyote, I waited until the beast was well out of sight before I ventured out to fill the bird feeder.

> *The LORD is my light and my salvation — so why should I be afraid? The LORD is my fortress, protecting me from danger, so why should I tremble?*
> Psalm 27:1 NLT

Gold Cat used to show up quite frequently at our door for his breakfast bearing scars from the previous night's altercation with a raccoon, possum, or some other wild creature that roams in the darkness in search of prey. Though we many times had offered Gold Cat the safety of our home, the tom would have none of it, choosing a life of freedom despite its inherent dangers and need for constant watchfulness. Gold Cat in his strength was the quintessential tough guy who seemed to have never met a fight he didn't like.

For her part, Indy ran and hid whenever Gold Cat would come to the door for his handout. The other three indoor cats would draw back warily, perhaps knowing instinctively that this was one tough dude and no good would come of a challenge to his space on the porch. Gold Cat didn't care whether the other cats made him welcome or not—he just wanted his food, and he wanted it now.

On the bravery scale, most of us probably land somewhere between terrified Indy and fearless Gold Cat. While we can face down small worries and brush away shadowy fears, we wisely prefer safety to danger. The chance of falling into danger or meeting scary situations, however, remains a part of our lives, a point not lost on God.

> *Fear is a question: What are you afraid of, and why? Just as the seed of health is an illness, because illness contains information, our fears are a treasure house of self-knowledge if we explore them.*
> Marilyn Ferguson

When we're facing one of life's dangerous situations, whether major or minor, all-too-real or only worried about, God invites us to use the strength and power we have in him. We need not fear danger, nor are we required to take needless risks, but we can simply call on God in every circumstance, because the strength of his power and the safety of his love are always there for us.

Tazer

When Blake's teacher asked her students to write a story about someone or something important to them, Blake knew exactly what he wanted to write about. The seventh grader wanted to tell the story of Tazer, the small, skinny, scarred stray cat that had come into his life one day the year before and had taught him about birth and death, friendship and love.

One evening as Blake opened the back door to take the family's two dogs outside, the boy saw a cat dash across the yard into a hedge of dense bushes. Blake investigated and managed to coax a gray, white, and gold cat out of the bushes. She was mangy and thin and had scars from old wounds dotting the top of her head. Blake provided the cat with bowls of food and water. The cat was still there the next morning, so Blake provided more food. Jan and Jeff, Blake's parents, were not excited about adding a cat to the household, but they allowed Blake to keep the cat, and he named his new friend Tazer.

Jan and Blake took Tazer to the veterinarian to have her vaccinated and spayed or neutered, and that's when they learned Tazer was pregnant. Blake wrote in his story, "My mom cried" (though he didn't say whether his mother's tears stemmed from joy or despair), and a few weeks later, Tazer delivered a litter of four kittens in a box set up for her in the family's garage. Blake, who witnessed the birthing, was awestruck, but he noted "something wasn't right about one of the kittens."

> *Nobody who is not prepared to spoil cats will get from them the rewards that they are able to give those who will spoil them.*
> **Sir Compton Mackenzie**

One of Tazer's kittens was born with the umbilical cord wrapped around its foot, which cut off circulation and turned the foot white. "My dad got a scissors and proceeded to cut the umbilical cord and unwind it off its foot," Blake wrote, but days later the foot became loosened from its joint. The only way to save the kitten's life, their vet told the family, was to amputate the leg, so the operation was performed. The kitten's surgery healed quickly, and the kitten, minus one leg, returned home and soon started leaping and scampering with the rest of her littermates. "I learned a lot about how kittens are born," Blake wrote of this time, "and how to take care of them."

While Jan and Jeff agreed that Blake could keep Tazer, her kittens needed homes. One Sunday, Jan spread the word at church, and one by one, each of the kittens was taken, except the kitten with three legs. "We may just have to keep her," Jan said, "because no one's going to want her." That is, until one day late in the summer when Jan and her friend Belinda were sitting outside on Jan's deck, and the three-legged kitten began nudging Belinda's legs, begging for attention. Belinda's heart melted. "I'll be glad to take her," Belinda said as she picked up the enchanting kitten and wrapped the wriggly bundle in her arms. Tazer watched the scene with a great purr of satisfaction, then stretched out in the shade of the day lilies for a long, relaxed nap.

> *I give you peace, the kind of peace that only I can give. It isn't like the peace that this world can give. So don't be worried or afraid.*
> John 14:27 CEV

Under Blake's care, Tazer gained weight, developed a thick, glossy coat, and grew into a beautiful cat. "Tazer and I had an unbreakable friendship," Blake wrote in his essay. "I played with her for many hours every day. Tazer taught me about friendship and love." Blake continued his story:

"It was a cold December day, about three weeks before

Christmas. My mom accidentally ran over Tazer with the car." Tazer died in Jan's arms, and Jan wept in horror and heartbreak over what had happened. "We buried Tazer in the backyard," Blake wrote. "It felt like this was a bad dream and I didn't want to believe it. Tazer and I had been through a lot together. I had to learn how to face death."

Believe, when you are most unhappy, that there is something for you to do in the world. So long as you can sweeten another's pain, life is not in vain.
Helen Keller

For all lovers of cats, there comes a day when we need to say good-bye to one of our beloved feline friends, and those days are difficult, without question. Any one of us, though, who have learned something about love, joy, contentment, and comfort from our cat companions, would agree with Blake, who ended his essay with: "I was lucky to have her in my life."

The Meaning of Purr

Only when your consciousness is totally focused on the moment you are in can you receive whatever gift, lesson, or delight that moment has to offer.

Barbara De Angelis

To a cat, the human penchant for constant busyness must be puzzling. Cats yawn long and languorously without apology, and nap when they please without guilt. As we keep our anxious eyes on the clock, our cats keep contemplative eyes on us, wondering what could be so interesting about a clock's greenish digital squiggles. Perhaps we could learn something from our cats' perspective on time.

While I worked in the nine-to-five corporate world, most of my days consisted of going to the office in the morning, going home in the late afternoon, then going out again in the evening for a class or meeting. By the time I arrived back home at night, I'd be ready for bed. Weekends were taken up with housework, shopping, gardening, and church, and possibly a concert or dinner out with friends.

For the four cats of the family, watching me come and go must have been like trying to follow a tennis match as I bobbed from house to garage and garage to house every day. The daily time I spent with my cats, beyond a few minutes of greeting and petting, consisted of feeding them, grooming them, or playing with them. When a cat and I sat together, I had a book or newspaper in my hand, and my attention directed to the printed word.

I was satisfied, though, and I think the cats were, too. They had one another to keep them company, and I had the necessity of earning money for their food, their visits to the vet, and the roof over their heads.

Not until several years ago when I began working at home did I discover

Cats are rather delicate creatures and they are subject to a good many different ailments, but I have never heard of one who suffered from insomnia.
Joseph Wood Krutch

a new dimension of a cat's world. A cat is quite content to simply sit and enjoy the pleasure of the moment without doing anything else at all. No accompanying newspaper, book, music, project, or radio program is needed, as all these things detract from the experience and delight of being alive and breathing right now. Callie has been my main teacher in the art of pure relaxation.

When I sit down to read, as I like to do in the late afternoon, Callie comes right over to my chair. She circles it a few times, peers up to scan for the presence of any other cat, and if there's no squatter in the space, she jumps into my lap and commences a body-quivering, rumbling purr. Callie purrs and kneads, kneads and purrs, and it's impossible to continue reading in the presence of such concentrated pleasure. And why would I want my mind transported to another world and another time when Callie is finding such incredible delight in the here and now?

Teach us to number our days aright, that we may gain a heart of wisdom. . . . Satisfy us in the morning with your unfailing love, that we may sing for joy and be glad all our days.
Psalm 90:12, 14 NIV

Callie has coaxed me to put down my book for a few minutes and allow myself the experience of enjoying the moment. When I do, I study Callie's patchwork of curious markings and smile at God's creative whimsy, and I put my hand on her shoulders to feel the force of the cat's taut muscles as she works her front paws back and forth in rhythm with an ancestral pulse only she can hear.

I notice the sun's rays as they slant across the floor, and see that Cup has found her Eden in the soft warmth of a sunbeam, and that Indy is peacefully curled in the corner of another chair. Smokey wants in on the moment, too, so she scampers up the back of my chair and perches on the top, plopping her paws on my head. Callie looks up, only fleetingly distracted before she resumes her purring and kneading pleasure. *If you're willing to put down a good book for the sake of the moment, Callie says, I can ignore the pesky tortoiseshell.*

The days come and go like muffled and veiled figures sent from a distant friendly party, but they say nothing, and if we do not use the gifts they bring, they carry them as silently away.
Ralph Waldo Emerson

How long has it been since we've allowed ourselves to simply enjoy the moment? Many pleasures surround us—golden sunbeams, feathery clouds, a speck of stardust, the soft rub of our cat's face against our hands, the intricate detail of her markings. We need to balance our busy, active lives by taking cues from our cats and spend some time doing nothing except living for the magical miracle of the present moment.

63

Fur Your Consideration

Cats find malicious amusement in doing what they are
not wanted to do, and that with an affection of inno-
cence that materially aggravates
their deliberate offense.
Helen Winslow

When our own ill-considered words or actions mess up the pattern of our lives, we can't help but look back with some regret at having taken the course we did. Cats, however, never look back, they harbor no regret, and they worry not a moment about things such as messed-up pieces of anyone's grand design, even when the cats themselves are responsible for the mess.

Several years ago, I took up quilting in a big way. Inspired by a newspaper article about a couple who turned their formal dining room into a family media room, I decided to change our dining room into a sewing studio where I thought I could work my quilting projects without having to put away my sewing machine, fabric, and quilting frame every day. The transformation was successful, and I was delighted with my studio.

What I didn't take into account was the attraction quilting has for cats, and that the dining room has no doors. If Callie notices my quilting frame with my patchwork quilt stretched across its bars, she sees a hammock she can't resist and jumps into it for a nap. So I realized the need to dismantle the quilting frame whenever I'm not using it.

When I pull out my ever-growing stash of fabric from boxes and start sorting it by color, Indy, being a white cat, waits until I have a sufficient pile of dark colors, then stretches her body across it and begins to groom herself. When Indy is ready to lift herself off the pile of fabric, she leaves a layer of white cat fur behind. Rather than leave the fabric out to attract further attention, I put fabric back in boxes when I'm done for the day.

> *Perhaps it is because cats do not live by human patterns, do not fit themselves into prescribed behavior, that they are so united to creative people.*
> **Andre Norton**

Cup, the gray tabby, has a taste for pins and needles, so I need to make sure all pins are picked up from the floor and all pincushions, along with spools of thread, are put away in a cat-proof drawer.

Smokey likes to race into the room and jump up on my worktable when I'm in the middle of a project. One day, as I stood at my worktable arranging strips, squares, and triangles in preparation for stitching a sizable wallhanging, Smokey did her usual act of springing onto the table. In this case, pieces flew everywhere! Gold squares, red strips, green circles, and blue triangles scattered

As far as the east is from the west, so far does he remove our transgressions from us. As a father shows compassion to his children, so the LORD shows compassion to those who fear him.
Psalm 103:12–13 ESV

in the air like a celebratory hurrah and drifted down to cover the floor like confetti after a parade. Smokey, momentarily astonished at her feat, settled down in the middle of the table with a particularly pleased expression on her face.

As I gathered my pieces off the floor and began the task of reconstructing my design, I reflected on the many times we humans mess up God's good designs. We do it with the same unknowing recklessness as Smokey when she scatters the pieces of a quilting design. We often misuse what God has given us, as Callie does when she jumps onto the quilt stretched across the bars of the quilting frame, as Indy does when she leaves a spread of white fur on black fabric, and as Cup does when she chews pins.

Yes, the cats have modified the way I use my sewing studio, but I still have my space dedicated to a craft I love, so the overall purpose for the room has not changed. And when Smokey scattered my design, it didn't occur to me to give up on the pattern, or on Smokey. I simply stroked her, gently lifted her down from the table, picked up the pieces and assembled the pattern a second time, and covered it with cookie sheets until I had a chance to stitch it together. The wall-hanging turned out beautifully.

> *Having harvested all the knowledge and wisdom we can from our mistakes and failures, we should put them behind us and go ahead.*
> **Edith Johnson**

The Bible says that before we were even conceived, God had a design, a pattern, in mind for us. He created us as unique persons, born in certain places on particular days and years. Although we might, from time to time, misuse one of his gifts or mess up a few pieces of our lives, God still holds the grand design. We can trust him to watch over the patterns of our lives, and everything will turn out beautifully.

An Old Warrior

*Come to Me, all you who labor and are
heavy laden, and I will give you rest. Take
My yoke upon you and learn from Me . . .
and you will find rest for your souls.*
Matthew 11:28–29 NKJV

When we're hurting, we often draw into ourselves. We're fearful of exposing our wounds, our weaknesses, our vulnerabilities to our friends and loved ones, even though these are the people most willing and able to help us. The story of Gold Cat, the warrior cat, shows that a wounded cat will often flee in fear rather than trust a helping hand.

In his fourteenth year, Eli, our tiger-striped cat, developed kidney problems, and with heavy hearts we took him to the vet for the last time. Shortly after that sad day, we looked outside and saw a tiger-striped kitten dash through the rose garden where we had buried Eli. "He looks just like Eli," my mother remarked. I agreed, but in my mourning for Eli, I ignored the kitten and didn't make any move to offer food or provide shelter for the little animal seen scampering through our yard.

Months passed, and "Eli's ghost" became a regular in our neighborhood, mooching food from whoever would give it to him, but refusing anyone's attempt to pet him or bring him inside. By the time I started feeding him and showing interest in giving him a home, he had grown from a thin kitten into a lean, fierce, and wily tom with bright orange markings and a notably piercing howl. Known on the block as Gold Cat, he was not interested in becoming a sissy indoor lap cat in anyone's home when he could prowl freely as king of the neighborhood.

> *The cat may disappear on its own errands, but sooner or later, it returns once again for a little while, to greet us with its own type of love.*
> **Lloyd Alexander**

While accident or injury cuts life short for most outdoor cats, Gold Cat was an exception. Wary of humans, even those who fed him regularly, Gold Cat avoided being captured, and the tom carried himself with the bravado he needed to intimidate lesser critters. Despite the occasions when he showed up with a bloodied paw, a nipped backside, or a frostbitten ear, Gold Cat lived on his own terms for years, feasting door to door, maintaining his place among the nighttime creatures, and taking his shelter in the nooks and crannies of the sheds, decks, and gardens of the neighborhood.

After about ten years as a warrior tom, Gold Cat began to mellow. Maybe he realized he had passed his prime and could no longer depend on beating all comers, or the wandering life had lost its luster—in either case, Gold Cat began to spend more and more of his time in one yard, then on one porch, then, at last, in one home, our neighbors' house, with two human companions. He accepts their touch and the salve they put on his wounds to heal them. Under his humans' care, Gold Cat is fed regularly, enjoys the comfort of safety and security, and knows what it's like to be petted, stroked, and loved.

When I pass by Gold Cat's home and see him in the window contentedly snoozing in the sunshine, I remember that this home has been open to him since kittenhood, but the cat chose to remain outside despite the dangers, battles, uncertainties, and constant vigilance necessary for survival. Everything inside—care, safety, nourishment, and love—had been open to Gold Cat all along, and all he had to do was cross the threshold, enter in, and curl up on a soft, warm pillow, and when the tom got tired enough of fighting, that's exactly what he did.

> *Be merciful to me, O God, be merciful to me! For my soul trusts in You; and in the shadow of Your wings I will make my refuge.*
> Psalm 57:1 NKJV

When life's battles leave you battle-scarred, weary, and tired of fighting, remember that God's door is open to you, as it has been all along. Go to him for balm to soothe your wounds, refreshment to calm your soul, and nourishment to strengthen your spirit. Let his power and protection cover you as you take your rest in the comfort, encouragement, and inspiration of the Bible and his promises to you. Why face one more battle, one more hardship, or one more problem on your own?

Love seeks no cause beyond itself and no fruit. It is its own fruit, its own enjoyment. I love because I love; I love that I may love.
Saint Bernard of Clairvaux

God provides friends, loved ones, and many others to help us handle life's battles. Among those closest to us and those throughout the community, we have the support and resources we need to live in safety and security and enjoy the comforts of friendship and fellowship. We can allow God to show us today what it means to be completely loved, cared for, and cared about, because we are.

Necessary Boundaries

During the years when income seemed to go nowhere but up and consumer goods were within almost everyone's reach, the value of thrift and self-control became the province of our elders who had lived through the Great Depression. The recent economic downturn, however, has brought the virtues of thrift and self-control back in focus, and we're learning to say no to ourselves. Sylvie, a lover of all cats, applied the lesson.

Sylvie, a widow, lived in a small house she shared with three indoor cats, and in her gardening shed outside, Sylvie sheltered an indeterminate number of strays that came for the food she put out for them each day.

When Sylvie left for work in the morning, the outdoor cats strolled over and rubbed themselves against her legs, stretching as Sylvie stroked their long, lean bodies from ears to tail. When she returned home, her indoor cats scampered to the door and nudged one another aside in their attempt to be first in line for Sylvie's attention. Like many humans whose lives are graced with the love of many cats, Sylvie told everyone, "These are my babies."

Sylvie earned a modest salary from her clerical position at a small trucking company, but she wanted little beyond her cats, and she spent most of her money on food and care for her feline friends. Many times over the years she had smiled in satisfaction at the surprisingly pleasant turn her life had taken since the loss of her beloved husband, when she fully believed she would never know happiness again.

> *There is nothing in the animal world, to my mind, more delightful than grown cats at play. They are so swift and light and graceful, so subtle and designing, and yet so richly comic.*
> **Monica Edwards**

One day, about the time the nation's economy became a staple of the nightly news, Sylvie was at work and noticed a photo of a kitten on the office bulletin board. "Free to Good Home" read the caption under the photo. Sylvie didn't need to read the kitten's description, because the face staring back at her was the image of Puff, her first cat. Memories of her sixth birthday and the fuzzy, squirmy white kitten Sylvie's mother set in the child's open arms overflowed Sylvie's heart. How wonderful it would be to take Puff's "twin"! And what's one more, anyway? Sylvie reached in her pocket for her cell to call the contact number, and then she stopped, her hand still resting on her phone.

Already rumors were circulating around the company concerning possible layoffs, and Sylvie's position was not immune to elimination. Another cat would mean another set of vaccinations to pay for, as well as more food and litter. And while her three indoor cats got along amicably, her house was small, and she wondered if one more cat would pose problems for all of them.

> *We know that for those who love God all things work together for good, for those who are called according to his purpose.*
> **Romans 8:28 ESV**

"Right now is not the time," Sylvie told herself, and she released the cell phone. She pictured her three cats at home dozing peacefully in the warmth of the noontime sun as it spilled through her living room window. She thought of her outdoor cats lying in the shade of her porch and patio, and her heart warmed in gratitude. "Instead of getting another," Sylvie vowed, "I'll take care of what I have."

Sylvie returned home that day, and several cats emerged from the lengthening shadows to follow her from the garage to her back door, and three feline faces greeted her as she stepped inside her house. The following day, Sylvie learned that a co-worker who was retiring adopted Puff, so human and kitten were ready to embark on a new stage in life. Sylvie, a lover of cats, was very satisfied.

> *Each day, and the living of it, has to be a conscious creation in which discipline and order are relieved with some play and pure foolishness.*
> **May Sarton**

Being able to say no to an added responsibility, another claim on our resources, to something our hearts desire, releases us to say yes to fully embracing the responsibilities we already have. As our elders knew before us, there's deep satisfaction and peace of mind in living within our financial, emotional, and physical means.

In whatever way the current economic troubles have touched our lives, we should remember God's ability to make good come out of bad. He has a way of turning loss to gain, setbacks to progress, experience to wisdom. With each no the economic situation may force us to say, let us recommit ourselves to living contentedly with what we have and in heartfelt gratitude for God's eternal and unchangeable yes.

Of all the toys available, none is better designed than the owner himself. A large multipurpose plaything, its parts can be made to move in almost any direction. It comes completely assembled, and it makes a sound when you jump on it.

Stephen Baker

Hidden in Plain View

It is a common experience that a problem difficult at night is resolved in the morning after the committee of sleep has worked on it.

John Steinbeck

When I'm feeling frustrated because I have a problem and I don't know how to fix it, I've learned that the best thing to do is nothing. Nothing, that is, until I've given myself a chance to relax, clear my thinking, and approach the problem from an angle apart from panic. After I've calmed down, I'm often surprised (and a little embarrassed) to realize that the solution has been evident all along.

My sister and brother-in-law live next door, so when they travel, I'm the neighbor in charge of visiting, feeding, and cleaning up after their two cats, Juno and Tabby. The cats are complete opposites in appearance and temperament.

Juno is a high-strung Siamese cat who's wary of anyone she meets except Janice and David, and the fact I'm family makes no difference to Juno. For several days after Janice and David leave for a trip, Juno greets me at the front door with a searing hiss and sharp nip to my ankle, and then she stands back and glares to make sure I understand her feelings. To the advice "Don't bite the hand that feeds you," Juno would contemptuously reply, *I don't bite anyone's hands. I go straight for ankles.*

> *Cats, as a class, have never completely got over the snootiness caused by the fact that in ancient Egypt they were worshipped as gods.*
> P. G. Wodehouse

Tabby, Juno's feline companion, is a gray and white cat, a stray that endeared herself to David by being an unassuming and gentle, affectionate, and quiet creature. Unlike Juno, Tabby welcomes the human touch without even so much as a passing thought of using her teeth or claws in response. When Janice and David go away, however, Tabby generally hides for a couple of days until a new routine has been established and Tabby decides it's safe to present herself.

Last year, while Janice and David traveled, I was seeing to my cat duties as usual. Three days or so after they left, Juno settled down, refraining from attacking me when I entered the house, and Tabby allowed me to see her, play with her, brush her, and pet her. The cats and I had reached a workable truce and things were going well. At the end of the week, however, I had a problem.

During my morning visit, I missed seeing Tabby. I took a look around, but I didn't worry because I knew Tabby liked to hide sometimes. I figured she was under a bed or behind the couch. Besides, Tabby's food dish was empty, a clear sign of her presence during the night, as Juno deemed Tabby's brand of cat food unfit for consumption. When I returned that evening, however, I still didn't see Tabby, and I became concerned, fearing she had gotten out, or was closed in a closet, or was sick and lying helpless someplace in the house. In the middle of the living room carpet, Juno sat like a regal, all-knowing sage, but no help to me at all. If Tabby had been a canary, I would have feared the worst.

> *If you don't know what you're doing, pray to the Father. He loves to help. You'll get his help, and won't be condescended to when you ask for it. Ask boldly, believingly, without a second thought.*
> James 1:5–6 MSG

I began a thorough search of the house, from Tabby's likely hiding places to highly improbable hiding places, such as down in the basement despite a firmly closed door at the top of the stairs. I searched a second time. Then, at my wit's end, I decided I might be scaring Tabby off with my increasingly frantic movement, so I stopped, lay down on Janice's chaise longue, and breathed calmly in hopes that Tabby might show up of her own accord.

For a few minutes, I closed my eyes. Then, when I opened my eyes, I saw Tabby. Right in my line of vision sat the cat, calm and collected, on a tapestry chair Janice had placed in a dimly lit corner of the room. Tabby blinked. So did I. I have no doubt whatsoever that the cat had been sitting in plain view all along, wondering why in the world I was running up and down stairs, from room to room, peering under beds and in closets.

> *Ninety-nine percent of problems are like sparks; they will burn out if they are not fanned. The early approach of leaders should be to keep conflicts calm.*
> **Leith Anderson**

In life, solutions have a way of sitting in plain view, although we may not find them if we insist on searching frantically for them. Solutions, like cats, present themselves to us only after we still our bodies, quiet our minds, and change our posture from one of frantic searching to one of humble reception. Perhaps that's why God recommends prayer when we need a solution to life's frustrations.

Serendipity

> *With the qualities of cleanliness, affection,*
> *patience, dignity, and courage that cats*
> *have, how many of us, I ask you, would*
> *be capable of becoming cats?*
>
> Fernand Mery

Through a friend's recommendation, Amy landed a plum project, one she hadn't even applied for. "Most good things in my life have come through serendipity," Amy said to her friend as the two women sipped coffee at their local Starbucks. Then Amy related to her friend the story of Serendipity, the cat that changed the life of a man she had known in college, a man who had become a crusty bachelor in his middle years.

Though they had lost track of each other after they graduated, Amy recognized Larry's name on a lengthy, didactic message he had posted to their university's alumni chat room. Amy, living several states away, responded to the post, and so began a series of private e-mails, with Larry defending his views on culture, religion, politics, and people and Amy challenging the statements she found particularly unproductive.

Best Friends Forever: Me and My Cat

In the course of Amy and Larry's correspondence, Amy learned that Larry lived alone in the carriage house of a large estate, took care of the property in exchange for rent, and worked in their college's admissions office. Since Larry seemed to have no family nearby and few friends, Amy made a point of keeping their e-mail correspondence going.

After a year of weekly exchanges, Amy received an e-mail from Larry that read: "Mangy yellow cat roaming the property. Can't stand cats, but it looked so pitiful I gave it a dish of gravy." Then Larry launched into the various reasons he hated cats, closing with the statement "That cat better scat."

> *It was difficult to be vexed by a creature that burst into a chorus of purring as soon as I spoke to him.*
> Philip Brown

The cat, however, had other plans. The next week, Amy learned that Larry, arriving home through a drenching rainstorm, spied the yellow cat huddled in a crevice near the front porch. "I let it in," Larry wrote. "Toweled it off. It can stay in tonight, but it's going outside tomorrow morning, rain or shine. I'm not having a beast tearing up the house while I'm at work."

Indeed, the cat spent the next day outside, but when Larry returned home, he found the cat waiting at his front door. "Cat walked in as if it owned the place," Larry reported to Amy, and then he launched into a diatribe about people who fail to spay or neuter their pets.

Several weeks later, Amy realized she had heard nothing from Larry, so she e-mailed him to ask how he was doing and about the yellow cat. "Cat's all right," Larry replied. "I've been giving her food, and her coat has a nice sheen to it now. She's fine in the house, never bothers a thing. By the way," Larry added, "I named her Serendipity. You know, a lot of things happen in life you don't expect or plan for, they're just seren-dipity." With that observation, Larry closed an unusually brief e-mail.

Better to be patient than powerful; better to have self-control than to conquer a city. We may throw the dice, but the LORD determines how they fall.
Proverbs 16:32–33
NLT

"Totally unlike Larry," Amy said to her friend as they both finished their coffee. "Then I noticed Larry's posts to the college Web site were shorter and less adamant, and I began to see another side of Larry. It's like he's getting back to the Larry I used to know—with his opinions, for sure, but fun to be around and not so tense. So I think Seren-dipity has changed his life for the better," Amy said as she and her friend got up to leave. "A cat can do that, you know!"

Amy's remark drew the two friends to talk about good things in their lives that had happened by serendipity. Amy mentioned how she met her future husband at a party she attended instead of staying home to study, because a professor had postponed an

> Every time we say, "I believe in the Holy Spirit," we mean that we believe that there is a living God able and willing to enter human personality and change it.
> J. B. Phillips

exam. Her friend noted how her career blossomed at a company she applied to only because a cousin of hers worked there, and that's where she met Amy. "So it's by serendipity we know each other," Amy said, "and your friendship has changed my life for the better."

"As yours has changed mine," her friend said, and the two hugged before parting.

If we think about those things that have changed our lives for the better, we may see a series of small events that came together, seemingly by serendipity, but maybe not. God, in his good time, sends the people and events (and cats) into our lives that he knows will bring blessings to us. Our lives are important to God, and he wouldn't leave anything to chance.

Lured by Love

*Love me, please, I love you; I can bear to be
your friend. So ask of me anything. . . . I
am not a tentative person. Whatever I do, I
give up my whole self to it.*
Edna St. Vincent Millay

The power of love is evident when a mother's compassion guides her struggling child through a difficult stage, or a teacher's kindness helps an angry student overcome negative habits and attitudes. When I realized that Callie resented having to share the house with other cats, I wondered if I could change her mind from jealousy to acceptance by showering her with love and attention.

The day I adopted Callie, the shelter attendant clicked through the shelter's computer files, found Callie's, and announced, "Callie was given up because her owner had too many cats. It says here Callie would be happier as an only cat." The information did nothing to deter me from adopting both Callie and Cup, as I believed our house large enough to offer both cats sufficient space to call their own. Besides, I thought both animals would appreciate the company of one of their own kind.

Once in the house, the first thing Callie did upon being released from her carrier was hiss at Cup, who ignored Callie and went about, nose first, exploring her new territory. In a short time, however, Callie accommodated herself to Cup, and the two cats seemed to get along well together, even sleeping side by side upon occasion.

> *A cat isn't fussy — just so long as you remember he likes his milk in the shallow, rose-patterned saucer and his fish on the blue plate, from which he will take it and eat it off the floor.*
> **Arthur Bridges**

After a year or so, two more cats came into the family, and Callie launched a serious protest. Jealous of any attention paid to one of the other cats, Callie stalked around with her tail low, let out muffled groans of irritation at the sight of one of the other cats, abandoned her usual sleeping and sitting places, and even withdrew from me, her favorite human. The shelter attendant's words came back to me: "She'd be happier as an only cat," and I knew she was right. I was responsible for Callie's obvious misery.

I had to do something about Callie's jealousy because each cat was now part of the family. I wondered if a human could change the perspective of a cat. Would it be possible to persuade Callie to at least tolerate the presence of the other cats? Because I wanted Callie to be happy again, I began a program of lavishing her with love in an attempt to show my love for her had not changed one bit. I wanted Callie to know there was nothing to be jealous about, and that there was plenty of love to go around.

First thing in the morning, I greeted, petted, and cuddled Callie before I looked at, least of all touched, another cat. During the day, I made a point to pick up Callie and hold her for a while, and whenever I heard her growling or hissing at one of the other cats, I rushed to give her attention, soothing her with strokes and assuring her with words of affection. At night, I put her up on my bed so she could be settled before another cat claimed the spot.

> *Place me like a seal over your heart, like a seal on your arm. For love is as strong as death, its jealousy as enduring as the grave. Love flashes like fire, the brightest kind of flame.*
> Song of Songs 8:6
> NLT

Over time, love did its job. As my extravagant expressions of preference for her became routine, Callie returned to her place in the household and among the cats, and now she rarely seems irritated at their presence. She frequently chooses to sit at a window or sleep on the sofa with one of her own kind right beside her. Maybe Callie would have preferred to live as an only cat, but with lavish love she has realized there's no reason to be jealous of anyone or any cat. In fact, from time to time I see Callie offer

> *When the satisfaction or the security of another person becomes as significant to one as one's own satisfaction or security, then the state of love exists.*
> Harry S. Sullivan

affectionate licks to one of her own kind!

We, too, sometimes let our emotions get the best of us, and we withdraw into depression if we feel we're not needed or loved anymore. Our willingness to lavish love—perhaps by listening, offering assurance, or providing practical assistance—can change lives. We will find out for ourselves when we realize our attention, our caring, and our extra love have brought smiles, confidence, and warmth to other hearts—hearts ready to pass on a little bit of that lavish love to others in need.

Diversity Training

There are diversities of gifts, but the same Spirit. There are differences of ministries, but the same Lord. And there are diversities of activities, but it is the same God who works all in all.

1 Corinthians 12:4–6 NKJV

Meghan, a seven-year-old, had heard her teachers and school counselors talk to her class about respecting people with backgrounds, families, and abilities different from hers. But Meghan learned the best lesson about diversity of gifts at home when Merlin, the British blue, joined the family. Laid-back Merlin was completely unlike the two eager-to-please, playful dogs that had been in Meghan's life ever since she could remember.

"We had the dogs before we had her," Meghan's mother told a neighbor, "so when Meghan wanted her own pet, we agreed she could pick out a kitten." Mother and daughter visited the animal shelter, and Meghan gravitated toward a big bundle of thick gray fur huddled in the corner of a kennel. Once the shelter volunteer opened the cage and placed the cat in Meghan's arms, the little girl wanted to look no further. Meghan buried her face in the cat's deep, soft coat and murmured, "I love you."

To Meghan's delight, the year-old cat, a British blue named Merlin, was brought home, taken to Meghan's room, and released from his carrier. Instead of jumping into Meghan's waiting arms, however, Merlin slid under Meghan's bed and huddled there, wide-eyed and worried. The dogs, sniffing at the closed door to Meghan's room, yipped and barked for attention. "You need to give Merlin time to adjust," Meghan's mother said, so they placed food, water, and a litter box in Meghan's bathroom, and left the room, closing the door behind them. That afternoon, Meghan took the dogs to the backyard and played catch with them, as she loved to do.

> *One can pick a cat to fit almost any kind of décor, color scheme, income, personality, mood. But under the fur, whatever the color it may be, there still lies, essentially unchanged, one of the world's free souls.*
> Eric Gurney

Merlin remained apart from the family for several weeks, preferring his spot under Meghan's bed to the risk of crossing the dogs elsewhere in the house. Meghan was disappointed in Merlin's lack of enthusiasm for play, and after a few days, the girl lost interest in the strange, silent being who didn't respond when called and had no desire to sit with the rest of the family or even come out from under the bed very often. Meghan wondered if it was even worthwhile having a cat.

In time, Merlin and the dogs reached an agreement that allowed Merlin to pass through the house unimpeded by the dogs' attention. Meghan, though she liked to stroke Merlin's lush fur, concluded that dogs were a lot more fun than cats—until the day one of the dogs destroyed Meghan's favorite stuffed bear.

It happened one morning when, before leaving for school, Meghan forgot to put her stuffed bear away. On that particular morning, Meghan's mother left the house for a quick errand without putting the dogs in their kennels. One of the dogs found the bear, and Meghan's mother came back to a pile of stuffing and shredded velour. When Meghan came home and saw what had happened, she was inconsolable. She ran to her room, scribbled a sign that read "Dogs Are Evil!" and taped the sign to her bedroom door. Then she shut herself in her room and cried.

> *The only accurate way to understand ourselves is by what God is and by what he does for us, not by what we are and what we do for him.*
> **Romans 12:3** MSG

Head buried in her hands, Meghan became aware of a gentle, moist nose touching her ears. Meghan lifted her head to see

Merlin's sweet eyes, full of concern. Merlin nudged her face and then licked the girl's tears as Meghan put her arms around Merlin's warm, soft body. Once again Meghan put her face in Merlin's rich coat and whispered, "I love you," as she took comfort in the cat's generous love and soothing warmth. From that day forward, Meghan realized that her dogs were fun to play with outside, but her cat was the special friend she could go to when she needed some quiet time,

> *Those talents which God has bestowed upon us are not our own goods but the free gifts of God; and any persons who become proud of them show their ungratefulness.*
> John Calvin

some comfort only a cat could give, and to share thoughts and dreams for just the two of them to know. "Both cats and dogs," Meghan decided, "are very good."

It's not hard to imagine that God says the same thing about us, seeing our many differences in personalities, skills, and interests as gifts we each can use to make the world "very good" for someone else. God doesn't ask any one of us to do everything, just the one thing we each do best.

Grandpa

You can't judge a book by its cover," the familiar adage says, and it's true, not only when it comes to people, but when it comes to cats, as well. Jean, a woman whose California backyard sheltered an ever-increasing number of the community's strays, learned that appearances don't tell the whole story when she discovered a gentle soul housed in the formidable bulk of a world-weary tom.

Jean never could turn away a hungry and homeless cat, and her home with its fenced yard and shady trees became a haven for strays. With the help of an animal welfare agency's free spay and neuter program, Jean had most of the animals fixed. But it wasn't uncommon for an already pregnant female to appear in Jean's yard looking for food, water, and shelter.

One day, a large gray and white tom ambled into Jean's yard. Unlike most of the strays, the tom didn't flinch when Jean approached him, and he allowed her to pet him and stroke his fur. Though weary and battle-worn, he was used to people and showed every sign of having been a house cat. Having found a comfortable place and a companionable person in charge, the tom made himself at home in Jean's yard. The other cats, perhaps eyeing his rough exterior, left him alone, and he, with the air of someone who has seen it all, paid no attention to the other guests.

> *The cat does not offer services. The cat offers itself. Of course he wants care and shelter. You don't buy love for nothing. Like all pure creatures, cats are practical.*
> William S. Burroughs

Shortly after the tom took up residence, a female cat whose belly drooped in the last stages of pregnancy slipped into the yard. Jean put a clean blanket and bowls of food and water in her old, unused doghouse and coaxed the expectant mom to go inside and make herself comfortable, which the shy cat did. A few days later, the cat delivered her litter of four sickly kittens.

The gray and white tom took notice, and he started edging closer and closer to the doghouse where Mama nursed her kits. As toms have been known to attack kittens, the gray and white cat's interest in the new family worried Jean. The mama cat, however, seemed unconcerned, even allowing the tom near enough to sniff her little brood; and the tom made no move to harm them.

After several weeks, Mama and the kittens' health began to improve, and Mama decided to take a stroll outside the doghouse. That's when Jean, to her horror, saw the gray and white tom enter the doghouse. Just as she was about to run outside to rescue the kittens, Jean realized the tom had settled himself down with the kittens clustered around him. She watched as he tenderly licked each one as they scampered up and down his mountain of fur.

"Whenever the mama cat would leave the kittens," Jean said, "that old tom would walk over and sit with them until she came back. From that day on, I called him Grandpa."

> *Jesus said, "Let the children come to me, and don't try to stop them! People who are like these children belong to God's kingdom."*
> Matthew 19:14 CEV

Grandpa remained with the transient population in Jean's yard until, for health reasons, it became obvious Jean needed to move into a smaller, more manageable home. The thought of leaving the outdoor cats to fend for themselves, however, filled her with overwhelming sadness, and she refused to move until other homes could be found for the current crop of cats. Fortunately, an animal welfare agency offered to help Jean move the strays to a no-kill shelter, where most were adopted.

Grandpa, the gray and white tom, was the exception. His heart for kittens and his loving nature earned him a place in a foster home for kittens. There, Grandpa lived out his days nurturing the kittens that were brought to the foster home until the kits were strong enough to be offered for adoption. Years later, when Jean heard about Grandpa's passing, she mourned the tough-looking tom with the tender heart. "I'll always picture that gentle cat," Jean said, "sitting happily watching over a passel of playful kittens."

> *You do not have to be rich to be generous. If you have the spirit of true generosity, a pauper can give like a prince.*
> Corinne U. Wells

It's only natural to make assumptions about a person based on appearance, but we're wise to withhold opinion. A sharp intellect, a creative mind, an elegant spirit, a compassionate heart aren't recognized by how a person looks, but by what a person does.

Head of the Household

When mothers and adult daughters opt to live under the same roof, they are bound to enter a period of adjustment as both learn the rules and expectations of their new relationship. My mother and I spent quite some time maneuvering back and forth before we reached the companionable equilibrium we enjoy today, and we can attribute a good part of our success to Eli, the orange-and-white-striped cat.

When we moved in together, my mother made it clear she did not want a cat in the house, but one day I was won over by a foundling kitten, a tiger-striped tom, in need of a home—our home. When I walked in the door with him, I hastily explained that the kitten, Eli, would stay in my room, a sunny and spacious place. There should be no conflict between Mom and the cat, and she definitely would not be burdened with its care. Mom eyed the scruffy, flea-bitten kitten with some disdain, but gave way to the fact there was now a cat in the house. I realized, though, that she saw in Eli's entrance an erosion of her parental authority.

In the space of a day, two flaws emerged in my idea of keeping Eli in my room while I was away at work. First, the cat liked neither a closed door nor being restricted to one room, however pleasant, and Eli tirelessly threw himself against the door in protest, creating a distressing racket. Second, my mother hated the thought of any animal being closed up, so she let Eli out before I came home.

> *Most of us rather like our cats to have a streak of wickedness. I should not feel quite easy in the company of any cat that walked about the house with a saintly expression.*
> Beverley Nichols

With the run of the house a given, we found that Eli was not particular about using the litter box, and clean-up obviously fell to the person home all day, my mother. Despite this and Eli's occasional biting fits, my mother refrained from saying, "I told you so." In fact, she and the cat bonded. Mom spoiled Eli with food, treats, and all-day, every-day companionship, and I realized Mom had the honor of being Eli's preferred person in the family. As Eli grew round and smug, I grew jealous of the relationship between my mother and him, feeling at times that she stole my cat, but Eli offered me enough of his attention to keep my envy under control. Besides, Eli's untamable, rude, and unruly antics provided me with a repertoire of stories, and the cat's notoriety spread among family, friends, and colleagues.

One day my sister arrived at our house with a gift. She proudly presented us with a refrigerator magnet in the shape of a big, round orange cat imprinted with the words "The head of the house is the one with the tail." We laughed and stuck the apt reminder to our refrigerator door. How well it suited our situation! Now neither one of us needed to jockey for position or worry about having the last word on anything, because the head of the household slot was filled by a hefty tom that never seemed to have a doubt about his authority.

> *There's a tremendous amount to be gained through what appears to be adversity. If we don't allow the crisis, these challenges to take place, then we remain fixed in life and never really ripen or mature.*
> Thomas More

After fourteen years of household dominance, Eli fell victim to kidney disease. That day signaled the end of an era for Mom and me, the era of Eli, the cat who was head of the household while our roles were changing. During his time with us, we were both navigating our new and different life stages, mine as a daughter wanting to be recognized as an adult, and Mom's as a senior forced to relinquish many of the responsibilities that had been hers and hers alone for so many decades.

99

While we're growing up, we often long to reach the next age, the next grade, to gain for ourselves the next privilege that will affirm our status as a big kid with clout. In early adulthood, we're eager to get out from under parental oversight, discover the world, and find out how we fit into it. By midlife, however, we realize there's yet another stage with its own necessities of taking on and letting go, embracing, rejoicing, forgiving, and accepting. For my mother and me, those years unfolded with understanding, mutual appreciation, and good humor because Eli the cat took his position as head of the household.

> *Acceptance says, "True, this is my situation at the moment. I'll look unblinkingly at the reality of it. But I'll also open my hands to accept willingly whatever a loving Father sends me."*
> Catherine Marshall

Charlie Comes Home

There is more happiness in heaven because of one sinner who turns to God than over ninety-nine good people who don't need to.

Luke 15:7 CEV

If you feel you would like to grow closer to God, you have reason to rejoice, because God desires to grow closer to you. It may not be easy for you to imagine God's delight when you turn to him, but Abby's story about a cat named Charlie and the delight of his human companion to see him home again helps illustrate the joyful reunion of God and one of his beloved children.

Mrs. Meyers told all the neighbors that her indoor-only cat, Charlie, had gotten out. "I've had houseguests," a visibly distraught Mrs. Meyers explained to Abby, who lived on her block, "and I guess with all the comings and goings, Charlie slipped out. He's never been outside, and I don't know if he's able to find his way home again." Abby promised she'd keep an eye out for Charlie, a brown Persian cat, most likely hungry, scared, and confused.

During the following week, Abby saw Mrs. Meyers walk around the neighborhood several times each day looking for her beloved Charlie. At each potential hiding place—a cluster of bushes, a sheltered patio—Mrs. Meyers called Charlie's name. Each day that passed brought a growing despair to the woman's gait and a deeper sadness to her voice. Nonetheless, Mrs. Meyers continued to walk and call and did not give up her search.

> *In the matter of animals I love only cats, but I love them unreasonably for their qualities and in spite of their numerous faults. I have only one, but I could not live without a cat.*
> Joris-Karl Huysmans

After Charlie had been gone a full week, Abby noticed her own cat sniffing at the window overlooking her front porch. As it wasn't unusual for a squirrel or passing dog to attract her cat's attention, Abby took little notice until her cat grew increasingly agitated, mewed, looked up at Abby, then back at the porch. Finally, Abby went to the window and followed the cat's gaze, but she saw nothing.

Hours later, Abby's cat still sat at the window. When Abby reentered the room, her cat again mewed, looked up at Abby, then back at the porch. This time Abby decided to step out onto the porch and see what might be causing her cat such anxiety. Doing so, Abby saw nothing but decided to water her large, leafy, and full-flowered potted plants while she was out on the porch anyway. She grabbed her watering can, filled it at the spigot, and set about spreading leaves and blossoms to reach the dark, rich soil with water.

Abby bent over her spectacular crimson-leafed caladium, parted its branches, but then jumped back in alarm to see two frightened gold eyes staring back at her. There, hovering in a fortress of decorative urns and leaves, sat the brown Persian cat, Charlie. He offered a mournful meow in greeting.

> *"We must celebrate with a feast, for this son of mine was dead and has now returned to life. He was lost, but now he is found."* So the party began. Luke 15:23–24 NLT

Abby gently set down her watering can and slowly pulled back the plant so she could reach Charlie, all the while talking to him soothingly in hopes he wouldn't dart away. Perhaps too tired and hungry to flee, Charlie allowed Abby to pick him up. Abby's cat pressed its face against the windowpane and meowed its approval.

It took Abby only a minute to get Charlie settled in her arms for the walk down the block to Mrs. Meyers' door. Abby rang the bell. Mrs. Meyers answered and gasped at what she saw as Abby poured the willing and appreciative Persian into Mrs. Meyers' outstretched arms. Joy and relief flooded her face. Mrs. Meyers had no words, only cries of pleasure as she nuzzled his soft, though now slightly scruffy, fur. Tears ran down her cheeks.

"To this day," Abby said, "I'm not sure Mrs. Meyers knows who it was that brought Charlie back, but it doesn't matter, really. All that matters is Charlie's home."

> *When we won't let ourselves be held in the midst of our messes by God who loves us and made us, we miss the unspeakable joy of knowing that we are truly His beloved.*
> Deborah Newman

Abby's story reflects the unbounded joy our heavenly Father expresses when he sees one of his children returning to him after a long absence. He opens the door wide. God asks no questions and needs no explanations, but instead reaches out his arms and draws each one close in a profound embrace. His face beams with delight because this beloved child, once lost, is home again.

From time to time all of us find ourselves away from our spiritual home, wandering aimlessly in unfamiliar or even frightening territory. It is at these times we can hear the voice of our heavenly Father calling for us as he reaches out to gather us back into the safety of his arms and his heart. When we're in him, we're truly at home.

Cats Know

We learn more by looking for the answer
to a question and not finding it than we
do from learning the answer itself.

Lloyd Alexander

With our limited human vocabulary, we may not ever understand the meaning of each meow and mew uttered by our cats, but we have good reason to believe our cats understand every word we speak, particularly if one of those words happens to be *vet* or *pill*. Mention one of these things and a cat's name in the same sentence, and the cat will instantly disappear from view.

The day before Cup was scheduled to visit the vet for her yearly shots, the vet's office called to confirm the appointment. While I had the receptionist on the line, I asked if I could bring in Indy, also.

Indy, getting on in years, has trouble clearing the mats that form in her long, cottony fur across her hindquarters, and she fights me when I try to brush them out. I knew from experience that the specialists at the vet's office are able to take care of her mats in minutes. "Sure," the receptionist said, "bring her in."

The next day, the day of the appointment, I brought out two carriers, and shortly before I was ready to leave, I started looking for Cup and Indy. It was our four cats' normal nap time, so I had no reason to anticipate a problem finding the two cats I wanted. I began looking in the obvious places.

Callie and Smokey were sleeping in plain sight, one on the sofa and the other on a chair, places I would expect to find them. When I walked into the room, those two cats didn't even look up. I continued onto the sun porch, a favorite room for cat naps, but neither Cup nor Indy was there. I went upstairs, and all beds were cat-free.

> *After scolding one's cat one looks into its face and is seized by the ugly suspicion that it understood every word. And has filed it for reference.*
> Charlotte Gray

I started looking under beds and in closets. I searched all chairs, backs of the chairs, tops of book-shelves, and under a table skirt. It was nearing time to leave, and the only two cats I could find were the two without an appointment at the vet. Callie and Smokey remained where they were, untroubled by my increasingly anxious mood and the presence of two open cat carriers.

I stood still for a few moments wondering what to do, when out of the corner of my eye I saw Cup slink downstairs and into the basement, a place she rarely goes. I didn't move, giving Cup a minute to settle herself, hoping I could disguise the fact that I was trying to catch her, and she would let me walk up to her. When I strolled down to the basement (quite casually, I thought), Cup had vanished.

I checked in between boxes of Christmas ornaments, under the workbench, and behind the washer and dryer. Then, on a shelf of art paper and poster board, I saw a flutter of movement. There was Cup, and, after some deft maneuvering, I was able to grab the cat and get her into her carrier. I tried one last look for Indy, but as I couldn't see her and time was running short, I gave up and left with Cup.

At the vet's, I apologized profusely to the specialist because I knew she had scheduled time for Indy. The specialist assured me she understood my dilemma with Indy's disappearance, which led to a general conversation among the clinicians about how cats seem to know when they have appointments at the vet. "But what I can't understand," I told them, "is that the two cats who had an appointment are the only two that disappeared. The other two went right on napping in plain sight."

> *Only God's Spirit gives new life. The Spirit is like the wind that blows wherever it wants to. You can hear the wind, but you don't know where it comes from or where it is going.*
> John 3:8 CEV

Someone joked that perhaps cats have ESP. Then the receptionist asked, "Was Indy in the room when you asked about bringing her in?" I thought about it and then said yes, she was sitting on the windowsill watching birds. The receptionist nodded knowingly. "That's it," she said. "Indy heard you talking."

At present you need to live the question. Perhaps you will gradually, without even noticing it, find yourself experiencing the answer, some distant day.
Rainer Maria Rilke

"Watch what you say around cats" is the practical lesson I learned from this experience, but the story reminds me, too, of how God's creation is full of spiritual questions that offer much to consider, much to ponder, questions we may never know the answers to until we're able to ask God himself.

Of all domestic animals, the cat is the most expressive. His face is capable of showing a wide range of expressions. His tail is a mirror of his mind. His gracefulness is surpassed only by his agility. And, along with all these, he has a sense of humor.

Walter Chandoha

Cat's Rebuke

When a cat is offended, every square centimeter of him is offended. Men and women of power and intellect have been brought to their knees by cats who have turned their backs on them.

A. P. Reilly

How we react to the whims and moods of a cat reflects our ability to accept with good humor and affectionate understanding the whims and moods of people—and even how we regard our own foibles, quirks, and eccentricities. I reflected on this as I listened to Brett tell me about how he endures the continued disdainful looks and turn-tail snubs of Salem, the family's little black cat.

"The stupid cat," Bob, Brett's dad, said as introduction to a story. Of the many Salem stories Bob has recounted over the years, not one has pointed to any sign of stupidity on the part of the cat. In fact, Salem seems quite smart to me. As I have pointed out to Bob, Salem knows that to get his breakfast at four-thirty in the morning, all she needs to do is walk back and forth across Bob's face until he gets up and feeds her, which he does.

Salem knows, too, that a person cannot read a newspaper with a black cat sprawled across the page, so Salem will lie across the newspaper whenever she wants Bob to stop reading and pay attention to her. Salem will leap at his legs whenever she wants Bob to play with her, even once tripping him on the stairway and causing Bob to break a rib and an arm in his fall. "Oops," I admitted at the hearing of that story, but even given Salem's responsibility for Bob's injuries, the cat could not be found stupid.

Bob's wife, Melvadean, and his adult son, Brett, both agreed Salem is not stupid. "But Salem doesn't like me," Brett said. "She hisses at me."

"What did you do to the cat to make Salem not like you and hiss at you?" I asked in mock accusation.

A cat's got her own opinion of human beings. She don't say much, but you can tell enough to make you anxious not to hear the whole of it.
Jerome K. Jerome

"Nothing!" Brett exclaimed, and then he proceeded to list all the good and caring things he does for Salem: feeds her, even at four-thirty in the morning, when his parents are away from home. Plays with her, or tries to, but the cat walks away. Brett gives her treats and attempts to pet her. "Salem rubs against my legs when I'm putting food in her dish, but once she has her food in front of her, she starts hissing at me again," Brett said as he laughed and threw his hands in the air.

"Salem hisses at me even when I'm simply walking past her. The cat never hisses at Mom or Dad," Brett added for emphasis, revealing that Salem is gender-neutral. "The dog, on the other hand, is different. Murphy keeps me company, comes running when I get out his leash, plays catch when I throw his ball. Murphy thinks I'm wonderful."

> *Know this, my beloved brothers: let every person be quick to hear, slow to speak, slow to anger; for the anger of man does not produce the righteousness of God.*
> James 1:19–20 ESV

I could offer no words of enlightenment as to why Salem snubs Brett, a handsome young man blessed with good humor and a caring heart. However, I can see a clear advantage this perplexing experience may bring to Brett. While the cat's assessment is less than flattering to him, Brett's good-humored tolerance of another's unexplainable actions and intractable behavior prepares him well for his other relationships.

If Brett's boss should decide to turn the workplace into a *Dilbert* cartoon strip, Brett will be able to laugh at the senseless directions and impossible goals of management. When he marries and his wife acts in a way deemed irrational by men, Brett will be able to accept the situation without criticism, which is a very wise course of action for men. Brett will know not to blame himself, take offense, or treat his wife with anything but consideration, because his self-confidence and his sense of humor will remain intact.

We're apt to take offense when we feel the sting of a friend's or loved one's careless words, dismissive behavior, or unexpected reaction. Our best defense is not to doubt our own worth, analyze or demonize the other, or grapple for logical reasons and clear explanations, but to accept ourselves and others with compassion, kindness, and good humor. After all, aren't we all at times like Salem the cat—whimsical, mysterious, quirky, irrational creatures going our own way for reasons we may not even know ourselves? Sometimes there's little to do in response but smile in recognition.

> *Keep your sense of humor. There's enough stress in the rest of your life to let bad shots ruin a game you're supposed to enjoy.*
> **Amy Alcott**

Freedom of Love

*If God is love, the more we can under-
stand the nature of love and put that
understanding into practice, the more
God-like will be our experience.*

Reginald Armor

W hen we truly love someone, we delight when our love is returned. A forced or coerced love would be a pale imitation and an ultimately unsatisfying substitute of love freely given to us out of the depths of our loved one's heart. As a girl, Sudha learned that true love requires free will when her cat Fancy could not be made to stay within the protecting walls of home.

Ten-year-old Sudha often accompanied her mother, a physician, when she visited patients in villages located near their hometown in northwest India. One day, while walking with her mother along a narrow village street, Sudha heard a pitiful meow coming from a garbage pile, then spotted a sickly black-and-white kitten foraging in the smelly refuse. "I glanced at Mom," Sudha recalled, "and she nodded yes. Because I thought her black-and-white fur was pretty, I named her Fancy."

Fancy lay cradled in Sudha's arms during the long, bumpy buggy ride back to the town where Sudha and her mother and father lived. Like other homes in India, Sudha's home was surrounded by a high wall designed to keep wild animals and trespassers out. "But the wall will not keep a cat in," Sudha's mother warned her daughter. "Cats roam where they wish and return when they wish."

As a kitten, Fancy was content to stay within the perimeters of the family compound's wall, but as she grew older, Fancy began to explore the world that lay outside the walls of Sudha's home.

When Fancy returned from her wanderings, usually the next morning, the cat howled loudly at the kitchen door for a plate of food, which she readily received from the family's kindhearted cook.

> *Of all God's creatures,*
> *there is only one that*
> *cannot be made slave*
> *of the leash. That*
> *one is the cat.*
> **Mark Twain**

One morning, however, Fancy didn't return to the kitchen as usual. Sudha was distraught at Fancy's absence, and when the following morning arrived with no sign of Fancy, Sudha and her mother looked around the neighborhood for the cat. Four days passed with Sudha continuing to search before and after school, but still no cat. Sudha's mother reminded her daughter of a cat's freedom to go where it pleases.

Then, late at night, Sudha woke to hear a plaintive meow at her window. She leaped out of bed to open the window, and in slipped Fancy, bruised, bleeding, and with brambles stuck to her damp and matted fur. Overcome with both joy and fright, Sudha cried out for her mother.

"In all probability," Sudha told me years later, "a wild cat had attacked her. Mom and I cleaned Fancy's wounds with warm water and antiseptic, and then Fancy lapped up a little milk. We wrapped her in her favorite blanket, then Mom put her in my arms and Fancy and I slept cuddled together for the rest of the night.

> *Trust steadily in God, hope unswervingly, love extravagantly. And the best of the three is love.*
> 1 Corinthians 13:13
> MSG

"The next morning, Mom had to go to work at the hospital, and I had to go to school, so we entrusted her to our cook, who promised not to let Fancy out of her sight."

Fancy's wounds healed, and the cat regained her strength. Soon Fancy returned to the cool tile floor for naps during the heat of the day and to the garden to chase sparrows, squirrels, and butterflies in the evening. One evening Sudha saw Fancy sitting on the top of the fence surrounding the property and contemplating the distance between the fence and the limb of a neighbor's tree. Sudha opened her mouth to call Fancy back from the wall, but she stopped when she remembered the truth of her mother's words about the nature of a cat to roam. It was then the girl realized that true love gives others the freedom to be who they are.

God's true love for us is the reason he never forces us to stay within the boundaries of his wishes and desires, though he certainly prefers to find us within the circle of his arms and the safety of his commandments. God invites us to stay where we can hear his voice, his call, his reassurance, and his promises, but when we stray God will go out to look for us and will wait for us to return. If we have been scarred and bloodied, he will heal us. Why? Because God has true love for us.

> *If love does not know how to give and take without restrictions, it is not love, but a transaction that never fails to lay stress on a plus and a minus.*
> Emma Goldman

Not Ready for Prime Time

The advent of reality TV has given everyone a chance
to get in front a camera, but by now, many of us have
found that perhaps not everyone should. When Eli, my
tiger-striped tom, and I had our chance at stardom, I
discovered that performing in the glare of a spotlight is
not as easy as it looks and that there are many hurdles
on the road to fame.

Eli came to me as a kitten rescued by a co-worker and brought
into the office for adoption. Since everyone in my department
knew I had taken the striped tom, Eli's exploits as a rambunctious
kitten and spoiled cat served as the subject of break-time conver-
sations for years.

One day our corporation's public relations department con-
tacted me about posing with Eli for a photo that would accom-

pany an article about pets and be included in a publicity packet sent to newspapers and other media outlets. I was delighted, as I believed Eli possessed the heft and personality of Morris the Cat, the famously finicky spokescat for 9Lives cat food. I imagined the photo would spring Eli (and me) from oblivion into fame.

The morning of our photo shoot, I got ready for work and put Eli in the cat carrier and in the car. For the first few miles of our drive, Eli yowled piteously, but by the time I pulled into the parking lot at work, he had hunkered down in his carrier, growling his displeasure and glaring in fear and suspicion.

I lifted the carrier out of the car, and the first hurdle on the road to fame presented itself in the long walk between the parking lot and the photo studio. Eli weighed close to twenty pounds, so by the time I reached the studio, I was drained. Nonetheless, we had a schedule to meet, so I opened the carrier, reached in for Eli, and encountered the second hurdle on the road to fame, as Eli did not want to budge. After I pulled him out, much against his will, the cat clung to me in sheer terror, his eyes wide as pie pans, his nostrils flared, and his legs taut with tension.

> *Cats assume their strangest, most intriguing and beautiful postures only when it is impossible to photograph them. Cat calendars disappoint because they show only the public range of cat positions.*
> J. R. Coulson

I positioned myself on a stool with my distressed cat, surrounded by at least half a dozen glaring pole lamps and a camera. Despite my best efforts to calm him, Eli struggled against the grip of my increasingly nervous and sweaty hands, and I worried what would happen if he should leap out of my arms and disappear into the cavernous studio filled with boxes, props, crates, and curtains.

Shortly, subdued by the heat and glare of the lamps, Eli stopped struggling, pulled his paws tight to his body, and sat defiantly on my lap like a heavy lump of fur with eyeballs. While the photographer adjusted, clicked, readjusted, clicked, and adjusted again, Eli's fur dampened into a dull flat mat, and I felt my shirt clinging to my body. The third hurdle on the road to fame, I realized, is just being able sit under bright lights without dissolving.

> *Not for our sake, GOD, no, not for our sake, but for your name's sake, show your glory.*
> Psalm 115:1 MSG

The photographer finished his work at last, and I took my exhausted cat back to his carrier. We went home, and for the next several mornings when I started getting ready for work, Eli made himself scarce, just to be sure I had no more projects on the calendar that included him.

The publicity materials were produced and distributed, though to little fanfare and no public acclaim. Perhaps the image of a terrorized tom in the clutches of a feverish-looking woman was not what the public relations people had in mind when they invited us to sit for a photo, and never again did anyone ask Eli or me to pose for pictures. Eli lived out his days in blissful obscurity, and I expect to do the same, despite the lure of televised singing contests and YouTube videos. I'm more than happy to let someone else take the spotlight.

> *Fame obviously has become a premium in everybody's life. Everybody thinks they deserve it, everybody thinks they want it and most people really don't enjoy it once they get it.*
> **Kelsey Grammer**

Even though many people continue to clamor for fame, life without a wide audience is still significant, vibrant, and valuable. If public admiration comes to us, we can praise God, and if it doesn't, we can praise God. We can give praise to God for being the people we are, famous or blessedly free of fame.

Ghost of a Chance

I think one of the reasons I married my husband
is that when he first came over he went straight
past me to say hello to my cat and dog.
I thought, this man's all right.

Nancy Pickard

For cat lovers, life-changing decisions often rest in the paws of a beloved bundle of fur. It happened this way when Holly, a cat companion, married Paul, also a cat companion. Both Holly and Paul found great happiness in being together, but the cats reacted differently. While Holly's cat found a lot to like in having Paul around, Paul's cat would have nothing to do with Holly.

Holly went to a breeder of Himalayans and found a feline companion by the name of Sebastian. From birth, Sebastian had received treatment befitting a prince, as he was the only surviving kitten from the litters of three mama cats pregnant at the same time. All three mamas nursed and groomed the pretty boy as their own. "He thought the world revolved around him," Holly said, and life with Holly did nothing to change Sebastian's high opinion of himself. An artist, Holly painted Sebastian's portrait at each stage of his kitten-hood and beyond, and Sebastian's likeness has hung in art shows and galleries, and graces cards and note paper that Holly sells.

Years after Sebastian's arrival in her home, Holly found herself in the enviable position of being courted by two men, both of them handsome, successful, and fun to be around. When it came time to make a decision about the one she wanted to share her life with, however, it was not a difficult choice. "One man had a cat," Holly said, "and the other was allergic to cats. Guess which one I married?"

A cat knows how to be comfortable, how to get the people around it to serve it. In a tranquil domestic situation, the cat is a veritable manipulative genius.
Roger Caras

Paul and Holly married, and the couple, along with Sebastian, the spoiled prince, and Paul's cat, Ghost, a pale yellow tiger stripe, formed the new family. Sebastian favored the new situation immediately. After all, he gained another pair of adoring hands to stroke his silky coat, serve his favorite treats, and scratch his tilted chin. Ghost, however, was of a different mind, as she was comfortable the way she had been and saw no need to change a thing. "As far as Ghost was concerned, I was the other woman," Holly said, "and Ghost would have nothing to do with me."

Ghost had ways of making her feelings clear, and one incident stands out in Holly's mind. Since Ghost was accustomed to riding in the car, Holly and Paul decided to take her along when they went on a short road trip. They also decided to drive Holly's car. Paul made Ghost her own spot in the backseat, and the couple settled the cat in and started out of town. Ghost, realizing an opportunity, promptly crouched in the corner of the backseat and used it as a litter box, an action soon apparent to those in the front seat. "She looked quite proud of herself," Holly said.

Seek not that the things which happen should happen as you wish; but wish the things which happen to be as they are, and you will have a tranquil flow of life.

Epictetus

Ghost treated Sebastian with more decorum, at least during the day. At night, however, each cat claimed its human, with Sebastian sleeping next to Holly on her side of the bed, and Ghost snuggling next to Paul on his side of the bed. If either cat dared to venture to the other side, a vicious fight broke out—not between Holly and Paul, but between Ghost and Sebastian. Eventually, the two cats reached a truce, and neither risked crossing over to the other side of the bed at night.

Despite Ghost's fanatic devotion to Paul and her refusal to accept Holly as part of the family, Holly added Ghost's portrait to the gallery of cats, and pictures of Ghost's soft gold-tipped face hang among those of Sebastian's regal countenance. The observant viewer, however, may count multiple pictures of Sebastian, the prince of Himalayans, basking comfortably in the sunshine of another heart to love him and two more hands to pamper him. Ghost, the cat who remains perturbed because she lost her exclusive claim to Paul's affections, claims fewer creative close-ups.

Times of change are times of fearfulness and times of opportunity. Which they may be for you depends upon your attitude toward them.
Ernest C. Wilson

Ghost's reaction reminds us to willingly step out of our comfort zone when new opportunities come our way. We open ourselves to fresh discoveries, to new sources of sunshine, and often to more love than we thought possible. Yes, our comfort zone may have been a good place, but there's always the chance that what's new will be even better. It's a matter of giving today a ghost of a chance to make us happy.

Little Bit

There was a definite process by which one made people into friends, and it involved talking to them and listening to them for hours at a time.

Rebecca West

A friend may lack the power to help you solve your problems, may not have the answers to life's tough questions, and may even lack the ability to completely understand what you are trying to say. But that friend's genuine care for who you are means more than anything else. When a stray kitten found Jean, the kitten found this kind of friend.

Every morning after she ate her breakfast on her patio, Jean brushed bread crumbs onto the ground for the birds to find. Jean enjoyed watching the flocks of birds that visited her front yard feast, and she gained a loyal chirping audience that perched in the trees anticipating a handout as she ate.

One morning, no birds flew down from the trees, even after Jean retreated into her house and sat quietly at the window with

her coffee cup in hand waiting for her visitors. It wasn't long before Jean discovered why: A kitten, crouched warily in the grass,
was nibbling at the bread crumbs. "Skinny and as big as a minute,"
Jean said, "and the poor thing licked up every single one of those
bread crumbs."

As Jean already housed two cats in her home, she was able to
fill a bowl with cat food for the scavenging animal, but as soon as the
patio door creaked open the kitten
darted off. Jean set the dish down on the
patio and slipped back inside the house.

*It is difficult to obtain
the friendship of a cat.
It is a philosophical
animal . . . one that
does not place its affec-
tions thoughtlessly.*
Théophile Gautier

About an hour later, the kitten re-
appeared and cautiously approached
the bowl, sniffed, and then buried its
face in it, gobbling the food down. As
soon as it cleaned the bowl, it dashed away, but returned the next
morning. And the next. Jean named the kitten Little Bit and continued putting out a fresh portion of food each morning and evening.
"I fed her for months before she would allow me to sit outside and
watch her eat," Jean said. "And when I was outside, I dared not
make a move, or she'd run off again."

One afternoon while Jean was puttering around her patio,
Little Bit suddenly appeared and moved closer to her than ever

before. Obviously agitated, Little Bit looked up at Jean, meowed, moved toward a neighbor's house, and then looked back to catch Jean's eye again. Jean followed Little Bit as the kitten led her to the neighbor's backyard and disappeared under a rarely moved trailer parked there.

> *Keep on loving each other as brothers. Do not forget to entertain strangers, for by so doing some people have entertained angels without knowing it.*
> Hebrews 13:1–2 NIV

In a few minutes, the neighbor appeared to find out why Jean was in his yard peering under his trailer. Once Jean explained, the young man crawled under the trailer in full expectation of finding a clutch of kittens, though after a thorough investigation, the young man found nothing under or around the trailer. There was nothing more to do. "I went home and sat back down on the bench in my yard," Jean said. "I sat there feeling so sorry for Little Bit because we couldn't find out what was bothering her. We just couldn't help her."

Then Little Bit appeared at Jean's feet and rubbed against her legs. After a few minutes, Little Bit jumped up on Jean's lap and began kneading and purring. "I stroked her with tears in my eyes," Jean said. "Even though I couldn't solve her problem, Little Bit knew I had tried my best to help, and from that moment we bonded." Little Bit joined Jean's two cats inside the house where the kitten grew and lived the rest of her days in safety, comfort, and contentment.

The people we trust, the people we call our friends, are not always able to solve our problems, but they do something perhaps far more valuable. Friends notice when things aren't going right. They take the time to ask what's wrong and listen while we share our worries and frustrations. Maybe there's nothing they can do to take away what's bothering us, and maybe they won't even completely understand what we're going through. But their compassion,

> *There is no wilderness like a life without friends; friendship multiplies blessings and minimizes misfortunes; it is a unique remedy against adversity, and it soothes the soul.*
> **Baltasar Gracián**

their presence, their readiness to help, and their willingness to walk with us a little distance along the road is something we never forget. These kinds of friends remain in our hearts forever.

No Ordinary Cat

I think I could turn and live with
animals, they are so placid and
self-contain'd, I stand and look
at them long and long.
Walt Whitman

Some people, just by walking into the room, attract the interest and attention of everyone there, while others can go through life largely unnoticed and often overlooked. It takes time to recognize the uniqueness of these quiet ones, just as it took time for me to appreciate the beauty of Cup, our plain and quiet cat, in contrast to her three feline housemates' flashier qualities.

Cup, a common gray-and-black-striped tabby with tidy short hair, came into our household as a playful and spirited kitten. Before long, though, Cup did what kittens do: She grew up to become a cat, developing into a husky matron, calm and sedate, plain and ordinary in appearance and demeanor. Only occasionally does she revert to her younger self by bristling her tail and darting from room to room for no apparent reason. These outbursts of energy dissipate quickly, however, and Cup settles back down to her routine, moving leisurely with the sunshine from the east side of the house to the west in search of the most hospitable place to take a nap. Cup is not a demanding cat, rarely asks for special attention, and outside her periodic outbursts, avoids calling attention to herself.

Next to the other three cats of the house, Cup blends into the background and seems happy to have it that way. The tabby boasts neither the quirky patchwork coat nor the touchy temperament of Callie, who is not above clamoring for my attention regardless of what I'm doing. Cup never asserts herself by jumping up on a visitor's lap and presenting her chin for scratching, as does Smokey, who is also known for sitting on the

> *If you really want to learn about life, get a cat. The way I think people should relate to animals is with a cat. Because the world is his.*
> **James Cromwell**

backs of upholstered chairs and playing in people's hair with her paws. Cup lacks the dainty frame, fluffy coat, and aristocratic demeanor of Indy, who always receives admiration from guests and accepts their praise as her due.

My sister frequently comments on Cup's plainness compared to the other cats, and especially to her own cat, a moody Siamese. When friends visit, they fuss over Callie, Smokey, and Indy, pointing out their distinctive appearances and personalities, while giving only cursory attention to the plain one, Cup. It's true that to most people Cup is just a common, ordinary cat. I, however, know differently.

One afternoon, Cup found me settled in her favorite chair by the window, and she quietly positioned herself next to me, box style, with her face lifted up like a sunflower to the sunshine. A soft shaft of light draped over her face and body, and I was captivated by the symmetry of the stripes curving across both sides of her chest and meeting in the middle, the intricate pattern painting her face, and the gemlike quality of her serene green eyes. Cup's coat took on the luster of silver and ebony, her design the handiwork of a rational, precise, and timeless Creator. While Callie, Smokey, and Indy each possess their own happy combination of colors and patterns, Cup is the epitome of order and rationality. How easy it is to overlook her beauty!

> *See how the lilies of the field grow. They do not labor or spin. Yet I tell you that not even Solomon in all his splendor was dressed like one of these.*
> Matthew 6:28–29 NIV

The same is true with people. I wonder how often I have overlooked someone who doesn't possess the gift of gab or an attention-grabbing personality, and in so doing missed the beauty of one of God's unique creations, someone imprinted with God's unmistakable signature, if only I had taken the time to look.

Maybe it takes some distance traveled along life's path to not only believe in one's own uniqueness but to actually see and appreciate the marvelous distinctive patterns of personalities, appearances, talents, and characteristics of others.

Some people are vibrant, eccentric, and immediately noticed for their offbeat humor and joie de vivre, while others are plain, unobtrusive, seemingly without anything to recommend

> *If a man doesn't delight in himself and the force in him and feel that he and it are wonders, how is all life to become important to him?*
> **Sherwood Anderson**

them. Yet I imagine God, who knows, sees, and loves us, finds each of us beautiful in our own way, with our own personality and pattern. He loves the splashy types among us as well as the quiet types. God our Creator adores each one of us just the way he made us.

Frank and a Friendship

You can make more friends in two months by
becoming interested in other people
than you can in two years by trying
to get other people interested in you.

Dale Carnegie

Most often, friendships develop not when people set out to make friends, but when they go about their day in kind, thoughtful, and friendly ways. Even small acts of caring and consideration are noticed and remembered, and kindness has a way of bringing people together. When Linda and Darrell opened their home to a kitten, they had no idea a new human friendship would follow!

The veterinarian knew Linda and Darrell well, as the couple had for many years brought in their elderly cat, Flash, for tests and treatment. When the time came for Flash to be put to sleep, their vet sympathized with Linda and Darrell, because he knew the couple would be returning to a home bereft of the presence of their beloved feline companion. That's why when another client, Ida, brought in a stray kitten in need of a home, the vet thought of Linda and Darrell first.

Ida had found the kitten near her house, crouched in the snow, cold and hungry. After picking him up, bringing him inside to her kitchen, wrapping him in a towel, and warming him against her body, Ida set down dishes of food and water for the animal, dishes belonging to her cat, Cleo.

As the little stranger eagerly lapped up the meal, Ida noted with pleasure the whimsical swirls of white and brown that floated across the tiny body, and she fell in love with the kitten immediately. The activity in the kitchen, however, brought another set of eyes, eyes noting these goings-on with no feelings of pleasure. Cleo sat in the doorway, surveying the scene.

Used to sharing neither her house nor her human with any other animal, Cleo crouched menacingly and began snarling at the interloper. The kitten stopped eating and stiffened in self-defense, his eyes darting from side to side in search of a place to hide, until Ida scooped him up and out of the way of danger. After weeks of rescuing the kitten, which she had named Frank, from Cleo's ominous threats, Ida knew she could not keep him. Frank, as much as she loved him,

> *Sometimes he sits at your feet looking into your face with an expression so gentle and caressing that the depth of this gaze startles you. Who can believe that there is no soul behind those luminous eyes!*
> Théophile Gautier

135

needed a home of his own. She took Frank to the vet and asked if he knew someone who might be interested in adopting him.

Darrell took the call from the vet's office, as Linda, a violinist with the symphony orchestra, was on tour at the time. Darrell said they might be interested but would wait until they both could visit, yet he dropped by the vet's office that day anyway just to peek at Frank. He called Linda. "I'd like you to see him," Darrell told his wife, and they agreed they'd definitely visit Frank as soon as Linda returned from tour.

> *Your kindness and love will always be with me each day of my life, and I will live forever in your house, Lord.*
> Psalm 23:6 CEV

The next day, Darrell went to see Frank once more, and that evening he talked to Linda again about the kitten, elaborating on Frank's looks, charm, and personality. "Why don't you go pick him up?" his wife asked, laughing. "I know I'll like him if you like him so much." The following morning, Darrell returned to the vet's office to pick up Frank.

When she arrived home, Linda was as thrilled as Darrell with the new member of their family. Linda took a photo of him in his new surroundings and penned a note "from Frank" to Ida, thanking her for her kindness in rescuing him and taking the time to find him a home. Linda delivered the note to the vet's office to be forwarded to Ida.

"Every year from then on," Linda said, "Ida sent Frank cards, along with a little toy, at Valentine's Day, Easter, and Christmas, and Frank wrote his thank-you notes and sent her pictures. You know," Linda added, "it developed into such a warm relationship. We finally met for coffee one day, and Ida was as friendly and kindhearted as Darrell and I had imagined. She's a wonderful friend, and we feel so blessed to know her."

Happiness is like a butterfly which, when pursued, is always beyond our grasp, but, if you will sit down quietly, may alight on you.
Nathaniel Hawthorne

So often friendships happen when we're simply going about our day, doing the things we do without any thought of advantage, return, or reimbursement. These are the friendships that seem to have a special blessing on them—a blessing reminding us of God's goodness, kindness, and care through the love and laughter of friends.

Ask Once, Ask Again

You decide what it is you want to accomplish and then you lay out your plans to get there, and then you just do it. It's pretty straightforward.

Nancy Ditz

Unlike humans, animals give no thought to developing complicated plans and devising intricate strategies to get what they want. Instead, animals simply ask by focusing on their need and persevering until they get what they're after. For both humans and animals, the direct approach and the willingness to ask and ask again most often bring success.

For Myra, it was an irritant. The skinny black-and-white cat darted back and forth in front of her car whenever she pulled out of her driveway and into the street on her way to work in the morning. For several days, Myra put down her car window, shooed the cat, and proceeded at a crawl until she could see the cat in the rearview mirror watching her as she drove away. Myra mentally checked off the neighboring houses as she continued her journey, none of which she believed harbored a cat allowed to roam at will. If the black-and-white cat was lost, Myra decided, one of the other families on the block would surely see it and give it a home, or the animal would move on to a more hospitable neighborhood. Myra had no plans of taking it in.

A week passed, and the black-and-white cat had not given up its dangerous game around the tires of Myra's car. Over the following weekend, Myra went from door to door in her neighborhood to ask if anyone was missing a black-and-white cat or knew

> *Cats speak a subtle language in which few sounds carry many meanings, depending on how they are sung or purred. "Mnrhnh" means comfortable soft chairs. It also means fish. It means genial companionship . . . and the absence of dogs.*
> Val Schaffner

where it lived. Not only did no one have a clue about where the cat might have come from, but no one else had seen it. "They began looking at me kind of strangely," Myra recalled.

On Monday morning, the black-and-white cat appeared and resumed darting back and forth across the street just as Myra was leaving her driveway. "This is it," Myra said as she pulled back into her driveway and parked the car. When she got out of the car, the black-and-white cat trotted up to her, rubbed against her legs, and then darted away, leaving Myra perplexed and standing in the driveway. Just as suddenly as the cat had left, the cat returned. Hanging from the cat's mouth was a scrawny, mewling black-and-white kitten. Myra sighed.

Myra raised the garage door, and the cat with her kitten trotted inside. When Myra opened the door to her kitchen, cat with kitten followed at her heels, Mama looking up at Myra with a look of eager expectancy mixed with profound gratitude. Before leaving for work, Myra put down water for the animals and closed off the kitchen. Returning from work late in the afternoon, Myra plopped down a bag of groceries on the kitchen counter—pouches of wet food, bags of dry food, and a canister of treats. "I wasn't sure what you'd like," she muttered to her waiting guests.

> *Keep on asking, and you will receive what you ask for. Keep on seeking, and you will find. Keep on knocking, and the door will be opened to you.*
> **Luke 11:9** NLT

By bedtime, any thoughts Myra had of finding another home for the cats had evaporated. Myra named the mama cat Suki, and Suki settled into the house to become a quiet, contented, and well-nourished matron. The kitten, Mike, grew out of kittenhood into a lean teen, guilty of pranks as diverse as peering out at Myra through the top branches of her Christmas tree to shredding the wallpaper on the wall behind her sofa.

Despite Mike's pranks, both cats became a cherished presence in Myra's home. She patted each one before she left in the morning, and she looked forward to seeing two black-and-white faces ready and eager to greet her as she stepped inside the house in the evening. "I guess I never would have brought in Suki if she hadn't been so persistent," Myra said with a smile. "And I'm so glad she was."

Emotional maturity is the ability to stick to a job and to struggle through until it is finished, to endure unpleasantness, discomfort and frustration.
Edward A. Strecker

God invites us to be persistent in asking him for the blessings he can give us, to be single-minded in bringing to him the desires of our hearts. So many times we don't have because we have never asked, and we never find because we have never looked. Let the story of Suki and Mike remind us to ask, and we will receive abundantly.

Happiness is like a cat. If you try to coax it or call it, it will avoid you; it will never come. But if you pay no attention to it and go about your business, you'll find it rubbing against your legs and jumping into your lap.

William Bennett

The Legacy

hildren learn about the world and how to go about living in it by watching the adults around them. More lasting than what we may say or what we may teach are the things children see us do every day over the course of weeks, months, and years. In a time of loss and sadness, little Brittany learned to embrace and protect something much smaller than she, her mother's beloved cat.

When Tom married Elaine, he gained not only an outgoing, attractive wife but also a sensitive Siamese cat. Elaine and her cat, Ling, were inseparable—"part of the bargain," as Elaine laughingly explained to her husband-to-be.

Ling adapted well to her new home and the company of another person in her human's life. When Brittany was born, Ling offered only token retaliation by clawing the back of an armchair, and then took Brittany's presence in stride.

Elaine left her job as a marketing director and enjoyed being a stay-at-home mom. When Elaine and the baby settled down for their daily nap, Ling stretched out beside Elaine and purred with contentment. With Ling looking on, Brittany went from crawling to walking to playing outside. Ling was at the door to greet them when Elaine and Brittany returned from grocery shopping, afternoon kindergarten, dance lessons, and play dates. A month after Brittany entered first grade, however, the family's routine changed abruptly. Elaine was diagnosed with a particularly virulent form of breast cancer.

"Would you tell me, please, which way I ought to go from here?" asked Alice. "That depends a good deal on where you want to get to," said the Cat.
Lewis Carroll

"Long before I realized anything was wrong," Elaine said later, "I noticed Ling was clingier than usual. She'd follow me around the house, even during her usual nap times. Whenever I would lie down, Ling would climb on my chest and begin kneading. *Ouch!* Unless there was a blanket between her claws and my skin, I'd have to move her off me!"

Treatment followed, and Brittany grew accustomed to coming home from school without her mother there to open the door for her. The little girl would go directly upstairs to her mother's bed, where Elaine and Ling would be sleeping. On those afternoons when her mother could not come downstairs, Brittany went back down to the kitchen to fill Ling's food bowl and freshen her water. It didn't take long for Ling to learn that Brittany's trip downstairs meant a meal.

Let no one despise your youth, but be an example to the believers in word, in conduct, in love, in spirit, in faith, in purity.
1 Timothy 4:12 NKJV

Elaine fought her cancer with passion and determination, but her body succumbed to the disease a year later. At church, Elaine's funeral drew a wide circle of family and friends, all offering what comfort they could to the distraught young father and his fearful little girl. Few eyes in the crowd around them could see Brittany without shedding tears for the child now bereft of her loving, energetic, and beautiful mother.

After the funeral and luncheon, Tom, along with Elaine's mother, took Brittany home, strangely empty without Elaine's presence. Ling had picked up on the new strangeness, too, because the cat did not appear at the door to greet the family as she usually did. She remained on the sofa with paws tucked tightly under, her tawny body tense, and her eyes watching warily.

Brittany saw Ling, walked over to her, and sat next to Ling on the sofa. Gently, Brittany pulled the compliant cat onto her lap. "Mommy was very sick, and now she has died," Brittany told the Siamese in a soothing voice. "Mommy loved you very much, and I do, too. So now I'm going to take care of you just the way Mommy did. I'll be here for you, Ling. You don't need to worry about anything." Brittany gave Ling a tender squeeze.

Lives of great men all remind us we can make our lives sublime, and, departing, leave behind us footprints on the sands of time.
Henry Wadsworth Longfellow

Ling seemed to understand. Late that night, she silently slipped into Brittany's room, jumped up on her bed, and gently settled herself next to the sleeping child.

The most valuable inheritance we can offer the next generation does not consist of money or possessions, but is something available for all of us to give, and that is an example of love and caring. When day to day we go about the business of our lives treating all living beings with kindness and compassion, when we live from the heart, we leave for the next generation a lasting legacy of love.

Angel's Gift

*Any glimpse into the life of an
animal quickens our own and
makes it so much the larger
and better in every way.*

John Muir

When the world of a child or teen suddenly turns upside down, the young person is left to work out confusing emotions and conflicting feelings. Sometimes the faithful presence of an animal can help the sensitive soul move forward, as Rachel found when a cat named Angel provided the teen with the stability she needed to help her through a difficult time in her life.

Rachel had just turned thirteen when her parents separated, and the change in her family left the child confused and fearful. She and her mother moved from the spacious home where Rachel grew up into a small rental in another neighborhood, and her mother's new job meant that Rachel would be home alone after school.

The girl hated entering the ghostly silence of an empty house, and the first thing she did after walking in the door was turn on the TV. After Rachel shrugged off her backpack, she went into the kitchen to fix a snack, when Angel, her mother's black-and-white cat, appeared and rubbed against her legs. Rachel ignored Angel until the cat's persistence forced her to fill her food bowl.

After her snack, Rachel went into her bedroom to do her homework, and Angel followed, claiming a corner of Rachel's desk. When Rachel left her books for her daily half hour of piano practice, Angel jumped to the top of the old upright and stretched out, listening in bliss as Rachel went through scales, exercises, and student pieces. As Angel's movements became more and more predictable, Rachel smiled, even announcing to the cat, "Okay, let's practice piano now."

> *Animals are reliable, many full of love, true in their affections, predictable in their actions, grateful and loyal. Difficult standards for people to live up to.*
> **Alfred A. Montapert**

Rachel's interest in writing led her to join the staff of the student newspaper during her first year of high school. As the term progressed, her growing circle of friends, her writing and music, and her academic achievements brought enrichment, structure, and happiness back into Rachel's young life.

Toward the end of Rachel's senior year in high school, Angel's health began to fail, and the cat did not respond to treatment. "At her age," the vet told Rachel's mother, "there's little else we can do outside experimental surgery." The expense of surgery and the obvious discomfort of the cat forced Rachel's mother to let Angel pass away peacefully in the loving arms of her daughter, who begged to hold the cat this last time.

After school the following day, Rachel unlocked the door of her home and entered as usual, but there was no *meow* to greet her at the door, and no leg rubs and purrs as she fixed her snack. The corner of Rachel's desk was empty, as was the top of the upright piano when Rachel sat down to practice. Rachel's tears fell as she lifted her hands to her face and wept.

> *It is good to give thanks to the LORD, to sing praises to your name, O Most High; to declare your steadfast love in the morning, and your faithfulness by night.*
> Psalm 92:1–2 ESV

Rachel returned to her desk and opened her laptop. In an article for the student newspaper, Rachel described the black-and-white cat that was a part of the family while she was growing up, a constant companion throughout her high school years, and that now was gone. "Life is precious," she wrote to her fellow students. "Don't take anything for granted, because you never know when it will be gone from your life. Give thanks for what you have each day."

Late the following summer, Rachel left for college, and after graduation, she and her college sweetheart married. Now the couple lives in a comfortable home with two young children, a black dog, and one big black-and-white cat that Rachel named Angel. "My Angel reminds me to appreciate the many angels I have in my life right now," Rachel said as she watched her children frolic with the dog. "She helps me remember to thank God each morning for my family, my friends, my home, and the lives of these wonderful pets that bring joy to all of us."

> *We inhabit ourselves without valuing ourselves, unable to see that here, now, this very moment is sacred; but once it's gone—its value is incontestable.*
> **Joyce Carol Oates**

The people, the cats, and the dogs are so much a part of life that we may be tempted to take them for granted. We need to take a few moments to name them and to give thanks for their presence in our lives, and for the sweet happiness of the memories they leave behind. Each one is a gift of the angels to us.

The Cat House

*Cat lovers can readily be identified. Their clothes al-
ways look old and well used. Their sheets look
like bath towels and their bath towels look
like a collection of knitting mistakes.*

Eric Gurney

Fully clawed cats and fragile home furnishings are incompatible. What cat companion has not put away a favorite vase, a cherished figurine, or a prized trophy to accommodate a pair of frisky kittens? Who has not, out of necessity, buried a gorgeous sofa under layers of frayed towels and ragged afghans to protect it from hair balls—or worse? Yes, a cat in the home significantly lowers your decorating standards.

The four cats we currently house came to us with all their claws intact and in full working order, and this fact determines our home's furnishings.

As our family's clawed population grew, I bought multiple scratching posts and planted them in strategic locations, such as by windows, on the sun porch, and next to the desk where I work.

Occasionally one of the cats will use a scratching post for the purpose of scratching, but no matter where I put a post, it fails to attract or satisfy a cat looking to sharpen her fingernails the way rugs and furniture can. In our house, rugs and furniture are cat magnets.

In my pre-cat years, I would have gasped at the nest of pulled wool I frequently find on the surface of my favorite living room rug. I would have panicked at the sight of loose threads hanging from the side of the sofa, and I would have died rather than allow a scratching post to take center stage in the living room. But not today. Not anymore. A sign of age, or maybe reality wore me out, but having a perfectly furnished and beautifully decorated home just isn't a priority, while the cats are, and there are positive things about the concessions cats make necessary.

> *The cat is the animal to whom the Creator gave the biggest eye, the softest fur, the most supremely delicate nostrils, a mobile ear, an unrivaled paw and a curved claw borrowed from the rose-tree.*
>
> Colette

Callie used to like to hook her claws into the eyelet lace of the bed skirt on my bed, so the bed skirt went. Now I see skirtless beds in home fashion magazines all the time, presented as a serene, modern look. Cup simply wouldn't leave the hall rugs alone, but insisted on bunching them up into a heap, so I took up the rugs and left the floor bare. Bare wood floors are beautiful, say room designers, and bare floors are much easier than rugs to keep clean, anyway.

Most of the changes, though, have taken place in the living room. The sofa cushions are covered with cat fur, and the sides of the sofa are fringed with threads. The one rug in the room is textured in ways the designer never intended, and only a few heavy bowls and vases sit on tables and shelves. A scratching post, rather than a decorative cabinet, sits by the window.

> *We fix our eyes not on what is seen, but on what is unseen. For what is seen is temporary, but what is unseen is eternal.*
> 2 Corinthians 4:18 NIV

Recently, a friend of mine came over to the house, and she looked around the room. "What happened?" she asked as she scanned my simplified, no-clutter style and caught sight of the rug. "The cats scratched the rugs, so except for this one, I eliminated them," I replied, pointing to the unfortunate rug. "The cats jump up on shelves, so I eliminated the breakables." Not one to mince words, my friend announced that she would have eliminated the cats.

Years ago, I loved to page through *House Beautiful* to glean ideas for colors, fabrics, and designs for our home, and now I consult the cats. What colors blend with cat fur? Which weaves remain reasonably intact after four pairs of claws have had a go at them? What designs camouflage stains? Because cats live in this house, my decorating priorities are not what they once were.

> *Besides the noble art of getting things done, there is the noble art of leaving things undone. The wisdom of life consists in the elimination of nonessentials.*
> Lin Yutang

Life's events and experiences have a way of changing our priorities as we move from one stage of life to another and our focus shifts from one set of needs to another. If we stubbornly cling to what at one time we thought we had to have to make us happy, we are not truly alive and responsive to the present. If we rigidly stick to old priorities, we deny an essential part of life, for life is about change.

By responding to our current circumstances, we develop flexibility and humor and nurture a spirit of acceptance and growth. It's freeing to follow new passions, new interests, and when needed, to reorder our priorities so they best serve God and the ones we love.

Here's Looking at You

A computer and a cat are somewhat alike —they
both purr, and like to be stroked, and spend
a lot of the day motionless. They also have
secrets they don't necessarily share.
John Updike

The eyes of love look past imperfections, and the
heart of love turns idiosyncrasies into endearing qualities. Such is the nature of genuine love in relationships
between two people, and also in relationships between
people and their cats. When I found Callie, she wasn't
a cat perfect in appearance, but the cat that was perfect
for me.

I loved Callie the moment I set eyes on her. Her willy-nilly
patchwork markings looked like the work of a quilter determined
to use every scrap of fabric, no matter what size or shape. The
sight of her pleading eyes and her pitifully thin frame, along with the
sound of her plaintive meow, made my heart melt, and I couldn't
wait to get Callie out of the animal shelter and into her forever
home with me. Once home, however, Callie's unique appearance
drew a range of unflattering comments.

"She looks mangy," my mother concluded as she watched the timid creature sniff her new surroundings. I couldn't deny the fact that Callie, obviously upset and unhappy in the shelter, had not been eating well or grooming herself.

"I've never seen markings quite like that," my sister said as she scrutinized the new arrival.

The next visitor announced outright, "That's the ugliest cat I've ever seen."

With a little time, appetizing food, and an agreeable environment, Callie lost her wretched appearance. Her frame filled out, and her coat took on the luster of a fine, robust cat. She began grooming herself carefully and regularly. The pattern of her patches, though, remained the same, and Callie to this day will draw quizzical glances.

> *There are people who reshape the world by force or argument, but the cat just lies there, dozing, and the world quietly reshapes itself to suit his comfort and convenience.*
> **Allen and Ivy Dodd**

I believe Callie's whimsically placed patches reflect God's sense of humor. Her face, a mix of black, white, and orange, is topped by two solid black ears. A black streak runs down her nose and mouth, and her white collar is punctuated by a black patch of fur below her chin. She has one white paw and three striped orange paws. A shaggy saddle of mottled black and orange drapes over her back and tail, and a mass of messy-looking white fur covers her chest and belly. Callie certainly doesn't meet beauty pageant standards, but let's face it, how many cats—or people—do? But to me, Callie meets my standards of beauty just the way she is.

Callie sits under my desk while I work at my computer, hops up in my lap while I read, and greets me at the door when I return to the house after being gone, even if I've been gone only as long as it takes to put the trash can out at the curb.

Perhaps because of the critical comments swirling around her when she first joined the family, Callie is easily offended and needs constant assurance of her worth, worthiness,

> *I am the world's Light. No one who follows me stumbles around in the darkness. I provide plenty of light to live in.*
> **John 8:12** MSG

and desirability; and she receives it from me. Daily I tell her what a good cat she is, how much I love her, and I praise her markings as the prettiest I've ever seen. And I mean it.

Callie's need for assurance and praise isn't so different from our need to hear from one another that we're looking good, we're doing well, we're making a difference to someone, and we're loved just the way we are. Truthfully, none of us are perfect, and it's a shame when we allow our real or perceived flaws to bring us down

You will find as you look back upon your life that the moments when you have really lived are the moments when you have done things in the spirit of love.
Henry Drummond

in our own eyes or in the eyes of others. It's a shame, too, when the flaws we see in others cloud our opinion of them, and we shower them with criticism instead of compliments.

It's helpful to remember, especially when we're feeling down about ourselves, that God is not criticizing us, but loves us just the way we are. He made each one of us different, so he's not measuring anyone against someone else, or holding any kind of contest meant to elevate some and lower others. No, he looks at us through the eyes of love, and he sees us as perfect for him, and perfect for doing everything he has in mind for us to do.

Mew Mew, the Military Cat

Unless we give part of ourselves away, unless we can live with other people and understand them and help them, we are missing the most essential part of our own lives.

Harold Taylor

Men and women in the military give up comforts the rest of us take for granted, but one of those comforts shouldn't be the love and companionship of a pet. Service members without a family at home, however, can adopt an animal without hesitation only if someone is willing and able to keep their pet when duty takes them away, and it's not always easy to find a loving and trusted temporary home.

When Regina, a member of the military stationed at Fort Leavenworth in Kansas, heard about two kittens that had been abandoned on the base, she went to see the woman who had taken in the kittens and was now looking for adoptive homes for them. Of the two frisky fellows at the woman's house, Regina fell in love with the gray and white one, an endearing, affectionate, and playful bundle of fur.

Regina happily took the kitten to her home on base and named him Mew Mew. Mew Mew grew from a frolicking youngster into a faithful companion who could be counted on to welcome Regina home at the end of each day with a leg rub, purr, and burbling mew-mew.

In 2004, Regina received an assignment that would keep her in Iraq for a year, and a woman she knew who had a dog grooming business offered to let Mew Mew stay with her while Regina was gone. Regina accepted the offer and said a tearful good-bye to Mew Mew, then went to Iraq, leaving her beloved pet in the woman's care.

> *Cats just purr. It's soothing to have a cat around. I like cats because I think they're funny; they give me one good laugh every day.*
> **Barbara Paul**

A year later, Regina, having completed her deployment, returned home excited to get Mew Mew back again, but she was heartbroken when she picked up her cat and found him infested with fleas. The woman in whose care she had left Mew Mew had handed him off to another person, and Mew Mew had been living in a flea-infested, multicat household. Regina felt terrible for having put Mew Mew through such an ordeal, and she felt let down because the woman did not do as she had promised.

Regina happened to relate the story of Mew Mew's sad

experience and her frustration to her friends Bob and Melvadean, both animal lovers. "Next time you're deployed," Melvadean told Regina, "you bring Mew Mew to our house, and we'll take care of him for you." Bob nodded in agreement.

Several times over the course of the following years, Regina was stationed around the country and frequently sent to places where she couldn't take Mew Mew, so the cat became a frequent guest in the home of Melvadean and Bob.

While the couple expected a period of adjustment each time they took him in, Mew Mew quickly adjusted to his temporary territory and change of routine, and he endeared himself to his hosts. "Mew Mew likes to get in your lap while you're in the recliner," Bob said, "and he starts kneading you with his paws, then he turns over so you can return the favor by rubbing his stomach." Melvadean added, "While I'm working on the computer, Mew Mew curls up in my lap and goes contentedly to sleep until I'm ready to get up."

Mew Mew's remarkable adaptability extends to Bob and Melvadean's dog and cat, too. While Mew Mew tends to ignore their dog, the two cats run, play, and wrestle, much to the enjoyment

> *Let us not grow weary while doing good, for in due season we shall reap if we do not lose heart. Therefore, as we have opportunity, let us do good to all.*
> **Galatians 6:9–10** NKJV

161

of Bob and Melvadean; spent, the cats sleep together curled in one tight circle of fur. "I believe Mew Mew would be at home anyplace in the world where there are people, food, and a place to sleep," Bob said with a chuckle. "We enjoy having Mew Mew so much that it's hard for us to give him up each time Regina comes back!"

Even if it's a little thing, do something for those who have need of help, something for which you get no pay but the privilege of doing it.
Albert Schweitzer

When she's away, Regina misses her cat's presence terribly, but it gives her needed peace of mind to know that Mew Mew is being well cared for, and most of all, loved.

Our willingness to keep, shelter, and love the pets of service members frees them to enjoy pets of their own at home and relieves them of worry about their animals' care and safety when away. What's more, like Bob and Melvadean, we as cat caregivers are likely to discover love and laughter in the presence of gentle, affectionate, and joy-bringing friends.

The Cat and the Sparrow

Cats are notoriously sore losers. Coming in second best, especially to someone as poorly coordinated as a human being, grates on their sensibility.

Stephen Baker

I'm thankful for a cat's predatory instincts when a mouse has gotten in the house, but I'm sorry when a bird falls prey to a well-fed outdoor cat. Though it's easy to feel compassion for the bird, the victim, I've found I can also empathize with the predator, because I know how easy it is to injure a sensitive spirit through careless words and actions.

Our neighbors' tiger-striped cat, Tabitha, joined their family several months ago, and Tabitha, an indoor/outdoor cat, enjoys romping across the lawn between our two houses.

One evening as I was drying dishes, I glanced out the kitchen window overlooking the lawn and noticed Tabitha in a state of intense excitement, crouching, pouncing, and leaping from side to side. The cat's body exuded tension, and she was singularly focused on something in the grass. What was she after? With the dish towel still in my hand, I stepped outside to get a closer look, hoping perhaps she had caught the mole that had made a maze of tunnels in the yard.

As I approached the cat, I realized Tabitha had caught a sparrow, and the bird was still alive. I stepped between Tabitha and her prey, and the cat arched her back, hissed, crouched down, backed up slightly, and glared. If a cat is able to shoot daggers with her eyes, Tabitha did, furious with me, this big human, taking advantage of a little cat's hunting prowess, surely seeking to claim as her own this excellent prize.

> *The cat has been described as the most perfect animal, the acme of muscular perfection and the supreme example in the animal kingdom of the coordination of mind and muscle.*
> Roseanne Ambrose-Brown

I was hoping that, once shielded from the cat, the bird would fly away, but when it didn't, I bent down to examine the bird. Tabitha took stock of my every motion. In an attempt to encourage the sparrow to fly away, I gently swooshed it with my dish towel. The bird hopped a little distance away, but it didn't seem able to attempt to flap its wings. I followed it, wondering if its wings were broken, though I couldn't see evidence of an injury.

Tabitha, slouching low in the grass, slowly and silently crept closer to the bird, but I continued to stand guard between predator and prey. The bird hopped another distance across the lawn, and after several minutes and another burst of energy, the bird made it to the other side of the house.

I now swished my dish towel at Tabitha, urging her to stay away and not follow the bird's path. Realizing herself outmaneuvered, Tabitha relaxed her body, settled herself in the flower bed, tucked her paws under her, and looked away from the sparrow, as if to say, *What bird? Who's interested in a bird?* The cat's face was the picture of innocence.

> *Aren't two sparrows sold for only a penny? But your Father knows when any one of them falls to the ground.*
> Matthew 10:29 CEV

I stayed and watched as the bird hopped onto one of the lower branches of a pine tree, where she found some measure of protection nestled in the evergreen's long, spiky needles. I returned to the kitchen and my dishes. I hope the bird recovered from her ordeal with cat, human, and dish towel, regained strength, and flew back to the safety of the skies. Tabitha, at any rate, slowly sauntered back to her house as if nothing of note had happened that evening.

When we're wronged, injured, or frightened by forces greater than ourselves, we can identify with the sparrow. Jesus' assurance of God's full knowledge of what has happened to us brings comfort because no matter how hurt we may be, we know we're not unnoticed and forgotten, but comforted and cared for.

If we're willing to admit it to ourselves, we also can identify with the cat. At times we've been the predator, bringing hardship or injury on someone else, whether by intention or accident. God is aware of those times, too. That's why he reaches out to us not only with comfort and care, but with forgiveness and love, separating us from our wrongs and bringing us close to himself. In him, we have the gift of genuine innocence.

> *In the time we have it is surely our duty to do all the good we can to all the people we can in all the ways we can.*
> William Barclay

As long as a sparrow falls to the ground and a cat stalks her prey, that's as long as God will be there to soothe and strengthen us, to cleanse and embrace us. He will be there for us every day.

Pleased As Purr

*They purr to signal a relaxed mood. And their
purring may also help relax them and those
around them who feel and hear their purring—like getting a nice massage in sound.*

Michael W. Fox

When we meet someone who greets each day with a heart of gratitude, who finds delight in ordinary things, and who overlooks minor vexations, we know we've met someone special. And when these traits describe a cat, we can be sure we're making the acquaintance of a most unusual feline! After all, cats are supposed to be haughty, snobby, and persnickety, aren't they?

Unlike our three cats that came from a shelter, the fourth, Smokey, came to us. As a stray, the tortoiseshell appeared at our kitchen window one morning, hopped inside, and made herself at home. We don't know where she came from or how it is she chose our house, but we're glad she did, because she's an especially affectionate and well-mannered cat. For her part, Smokey seems pleased with her choice, and she shows her pleasure in several ways.

First, Smokey never forgets to say thank-you for her food. At breakfast time, while her feline companions saunter to their food bowl as if they may or may not deign to sample its contents, Smokey dashes ahead of me into the kitchen and leaps up onto the counter, her tail quivering in exaltation against the cupboard door where her pouches of moist food are kept. Her body tenses with excitement as I reach for a pouch and tear it open. She dives into eating as soon as the tiny, moist morsels hit the plate, lapping until she cleans the dish, then sits back and grooms herself in a shaft of morning sunlight.

> *Cats can be cooperative when something feels good, which, to a cat, is the way everything is supposed to feel as much of the time as possible.*
> **Roger Caras**

Second, this cat is willing to let me brush her every day. When she sees me pick up the brush, Smokey stretches out, and as I brush, she rolls over at intervals while I sweep long strokes down back, sides, and belly. She kneads the air and purrs in ecstasy. The other cats? If they're not in the mood to be brushed, and they usually aren't, they refuse to sit still for a brushing.

Third, Smokey does something else none of the other cats in this household will do. She allows herself to be moved from one spot to another, and she holds no grudge against the person who moves her. When Smokey is taking her nap on the chair my sister usually sits in when she comes over to visit, my sister picks Smokey up, sits down, and sets the cat in her lap. Rather than indignantly jump off and walk away, Smokey simply looks up, shapes herself to the new surface, and purrs her pleasure until she falls asleep again.

The same holds true at bedtime. When my bed is occupied by sleeping cats and I disturb one by slipping under the covers and extending my legs, if the cat is any but Smokey, the disturbed cat will pop its head up, glare, hop off the bed in a huff, and settle elsewhere. If I disturb Smokey by getting into my own bed, she's cool. She'll stand up, assess the new landscape, mold her body to it, and go right back to sleep.

> *I will greatly rejoice in the LORD, my soul shall be joyful in my God; for He has clothed me with the garments of salvation, He has covered me with the robe of righteousness.*
> **Isaiah 61:10** NKJV

Smokey has found a happy and graceful way to live, and her example is worth emulating. She shows heartfelt gratitude for the blessing of food. How often do we remember to receive our daily meals, not only with gratitude, but with excitement? We're eating today, and thank you, God! Not everyone in this world can truthfully say those same words each day.

Smokey finds pleasure in ordinary activities, in the feel of the brush against her skin, and she delights in simple, everyday things. She walks with her tail high and watches the goings-on in the garden with interest. How many of us respond with amazement that we can get from one room to the other, comb our hair, and reach in the closet for a pair of jeans? Yet all these miracles of mind and muscle are amazing things to consider.

> *We must not wish anything other than what happens from moment to moment, all the while, however, exercising ourselves in goodness.*
> **Saint Catherine of Genoa**

Smokey's agreeable ways make her a particularly likable cat and pleasant companion. She's like a friend who is glad to see us, who finds something of interest to share, and who has a heart of genuine goodwill for everyone. She's pleasing as purr to be around—and it's pleasing as purr to others when we're that kind of friend.

The Blessing of Cats

These are the stories that never, never die,
that are carried like seed into a new coun-
try, are told to you and me and make
in us new and lasting strengths.
Meridel Le Sueur

Where is God? You've heard the cry in times of loss, when one beloved has passed away and left the grieving family behind. The question lingers in every grieving heart, and while none of us may ever hear the complete answer this side of heaven, the loss of Eli, the tiger-striped cat, gave me a glimpse into what might be a part of God's response when we ask, "Where is God?"

Eli, an orange-striped cat, came into our home as an eight-week-old kitten, and within a minuscule amount of time, Eli had his human family tightly wrapped around his little paw. He was a tom who, despite his undocumented early kittenhood, had never known the ways of the wild, yet he seemed to carry an ancestral memory of roaming his territory and marking it as his own. The rooms, the corners, the carpets of our house were over the course of time claimed as only a male cat can do.

After fourteen years of living life his own way and getting his own way, the formerly hefty tom started to lose weight, and his thick fur of earlier times thinned and dulled. Eli began to look out onto the world with still and thoughtful eyes, very different from the darting glances and dare-all-comers stance of the past. We took him to the vet, who diagnosed kidney disease. With medication, we were able to provide Eli with several months more of life, but the day came when it was obvious, out of compassion for the cat's suffering, we needed to say good-bye. Shortly afterward, however, a new cat, a senior cat in need of a home, entered our lives.

> *No amount of time can erase the memory of a good cat, and no amount of masking tape can ever totally remove his fur from your couch.*
> Leo Dworken

As his previous family was moving and could no longer keep him, we took in Merlin, a remarkably beautiful British blue. This pedigreed cat stood in stark contrast to Eli, whose alley ancestry could not be denied. Unfortunately, Merlin's lineage did not bring him a stable life, and he had been handed from one home to another over the course of his years. By the time he joined us, Merlin wore the look of the hopeless, afraid to trust the permanence of any person, place, or situation. Merlin accepted our care and shelter with a ghostly, resigned silence, an emotional stillness we tried to melt away with love and affection. We like to think he appreciated our efforts, and maybe even found some comfort in them, until his natural end came.

After Merlin's passing, our house seemed vacant without a feline presence, and we were in favor of opening our home to another cat that needed one. When my brother and I went to visit the shelter, one cat turned into two—Callie and Cup.

When Callie and Cup arrived in our home, we realized that as much as we missed rowdy Eli and regretted the passing of sweet Merlin, Callie and Cup brought with them new voices, new personalities, new adventures to discover. Without the open door left

> *I tell you the truth, unless a kernel of wheat is planted in the soil and dies, it remains alone. But its death will produce many new kernels—a plentiful harvest of new lives.*
> John 12:24 NLT

by their predecessors, we would never have known the joy of these two cats. My mother and I like to muse that if Eli and Merlin could look from where they rest in our garden and see the two new cats' faces at the window looking out over the spring-green lawn, they would wave a paw and wish the two newbies a happy life. Maybe Eli and Merlin might even share a story about the two women of the house who will care for them, shelter them, and cater to their every whim and desire.

Endings—saying good-bye to a beloved cat companion—are difficult and heartbreaking, yet without endings, we would never know beginnings. The circle of life would be stunted, the seasons of life only a dream or a concept. It's true, the faces, the voices, the personalities, and the purrs that have gone before cannot be replaced, and the presence of each beloved cat will never leave our hearts. New beginnings, however, show us how much bigger love can grow, how much more of life and joy we can embrace, and how many new blessings God has to give through the seasons of summer, fall, winter, and spring.

> *Help us to be ever faithful gardeners of the spirit, who know that without darkness nothing comes to birth, and without light nothing flowers.*
> May Sarton

A kitten is so flexible that she is almost double; the hind parts are equivalent to another kitten with which the forepart plays. She does not discover that her tail belongs to her until you tread on it.

Henry David Thoreau